MW01247570

GET INSPIRED

Fuel Your Startup with Your Passion and Purpose

Janine Lang

Practical Lessons and Tips
From Over Two Decades of Startup Coaching

Copyright ©2024 by Agile Business Planning, Corp.
For permission requests, speaking inquiries, and bulk order purchase options, email agilebusinssplanning@gmail.com.
Printed in the United States of America

Cover and Interior Design by Katie MJ
Author Photo by Dimitry

All rights reserved. No part of this book may be reproduced by any mechanical, photographic, or electronic process, or in the form of a phonographic recording, nor may it be stored in a retrieval system, transmitted, or otherwise copied for public or private use—other than for "fair use" as brief quotations embodied in articles and reviews—without prior written permission of the publisher.
This is a work of nonfiction. Nonetheless, the names, personal characteristic of individuals, and details of events have been changed in order to disguise identities or protect the privacy of the author's clients. Any resulting resemblance to persons living or dead is entirely coincidental and unintentional. The author of this book does not dispense financial, legal, or medical advice or prescribe the use of any technique, either directly or indirectly, as a form of treatment. The author's intent is only to offer information of a general nature to help you in your pursuit of discovering your passion, purpose, and polar star. In the event you use any of the information in this book, the author and publisher assume no responsibility for your actions.

Library of Congress Cataloging-in-Publication Data

Paperback ISBN: 978-1-0688233-2-9
Hardcover ISBN: 978-1-0688233-0-5
ebook ISBN: 978-1-0688233-1-2
Library of Congress Control Number: 2024911713

Dedicated to my father, who taught me unconditional love; my mother, who taught me resilience; and my sister Rose, who taught me compassion—all three who have sadly passed.

Table of Contents

Part C: Discovering Your Polar Star (Your Wish)

Part D: Wrapping Up

Introduction

There has never been a better time in history to start a business. According to Gallup research, approximately 60% of the global workforce is disengaged at work and therefore ready for a change."[1] One of the reasons for the high disengagement is a desire for more flexibility—many employees who experienced remote working during the COVID-19 lockdowns want the ability to continue to choose where and when they work.[2] Another reason for the disengagement is the desire for purpose or meaning in our jobs—employees who find themselves in a corporate position that is not aligned with their purpose will likely dream about starting a business.[3] Therefore it's no surprise we are seeing an unprecedented number of business registrations.

Who is the Intended Audience for This Book?

This book is written for individuals who are feeling stuck in their careers and considering starting a business as an alternative to full-time employment. The main character in this book is Alex Wong, a fictitious representation of many of the clients that I have had the privilege of coaching over the years. Alex, a 'corporate closet dreamer' who works in a job he hates, finds himself dreaming about the life he could have as a startup business owner. If you can relate to Alex's situation, this book is for you.

I decided to position Alex as an employee in the consulting sector for three main reasons. First, having spent over two decades in some of the largest consulting firms, I've noticed that the turnover of consulting professionals is high—it seems that someone leaves every week. Second, since most people who start up service-based businesses choose to provide some type of consulting service, such as finance, marketing, or human resources, I thought it would be helpful for the reader to learn about this sector. Finally, when I announced my plans to exit the corporate world to start a business, I was surprised at how many colleagues admitted that they had a similar dream. I'm hoping this book finds its way into their hands and the hands of people like them.

The secondary character in this book is Janine. And yes, I am Janine. The stories that she tells in the book are based on my own personal journey of starting two businesses and coaching entrepreneurs for two decades, which I openly share with my startup clients when I deliver my online courses.

How to Get Inspired for the Journey

The first step of the entrepreneurial journey is to foster the right mindset, which involves three shifts. The first mindset shift is **knowing your passion or your 'why.'** Thinking like an entrepreneur means that you are clear about why you want to start up a business or why the business you're creating must succeed. The reason why it is critical to know your compelling 'why' is because your commitment will be tested, again and again, and if you're not clear about why you're embarking on this journey, you will certainly one day quit when the going gets tough.

The second mindset shift is **discovering your purpose or your 'what.'** Thinking like an entrepreneur means you're able to describe your business idea or your vision for your business. Why is that important? When a startup owner lacks clarity about their purpose, they tend to drift along aimlessly, failing to make progress, which is tremendously discouraging.

I'm often asked whether startup owners should focus on their 'why' or their 'what' first. My answer is always to discover your 'why' first. When you have a compelling reason for achieving something important in your life, everything else will eventually fall into place. You will work hard at figuring out exactly what it is you want and how you will be able to achieve it. The secret to realizing your dream is to create a compelling enough reason for achieving it.

The third shift is to **discover your polar star or your 'wish.'** This is where you set a clear goal or target for your business. The significance of this element is that when we aren't clear about where we're headed, sadly we end up there—no place that excites us.

Unfortunately, most people struggle with fostering the right mindset. Barriers like fear of failure or success, imposter syndrome, staying stuck in an old identity, or limiting beliefs can get in the way of following through on a dream. There are also many myths and misperceptions about small business ownership that create unrealistic expectations for many startups, which can result in disappointment and defeatism when they're not met.

The Purpose of This Book

It's the unfortunate truth that 60% to 80% of startups will fail within the first few years.[4] The authors of the book *CEO Excellence: The Six Mindsets That Distinguish the Best Leaders from the Rest* uncovered the real answer to why most fail. According to the McKinsey partners Carolyn Dewar, Scott Keller, and Vikram Malhotra, the CEOs of these new businesses weren't prepared for the top job—they didn't really understand the work that they would be doing and as a result, it took them a while to figure things out."[5]

From my perspective, most jobs prepare you to be a specialist, to be a 'mile deep' in one area, whether that's finance, sales, marketing, IT, human resources, or some other profession. I believe that's why most people aren't prepared to step into the ultimate generalist role of having the 'top job.' Most corporate CEOs or startup owners will tell you that at some point they felt overwhelmed at the breadth of knowledge they needed to be successful in the role.

The purpose of this book is to prepare you, the startup owner, for your journey by educating you about the many common traps that people fall into when they are trying to make a shift from a corporate career to the life of a business owner. Most startup business owners courageously embark on an entrepreneurial journey in pursuit of their dream, unprepared for the battle and ultimately lose the war. GET INSPIRED is intended to prepare you to win the war and live your dream. I realize that sounds lofty, but that's why it's called a dream.

The Approach for the Book

Why did I decide to write a book about traps or failures? We learn more from our failures than our successes. In the words of Michael Jordan, "I've failed over and over and over again in my life. And that is why I succeed."[6]

Prepare yourself for the journey ahead by taking a copy of GET INSPIRED with you. I have packaged up the most common myths, mistakes and misperceptions that I've seen startups make, and captured the practical advice that I've provided to these clients to address them during my 20+ year career as a startup coach. My hope is that you will recognize these traps when you encounter them, and ideally avoid them. I do recognize that's not always realistic, so if you find yourself in the middle of one of these messes, my hope for you is that you fail fast and get up again quickly, building the resilience you need to persevere in your journey.

To enhance the readability of the book, I have added a summary at the end of each chapter that focuses on one of the ten lessons. The summary contains two sections:

Key Takeaways: This section provides you with the key learnings or the 'nuggets' that you will want to remember from the chapter to reinforce the learning.

Question to Ask: This section includes one or two questions that you can ask yourself to apply the learning to your own unique situation.

I hope this book will serve as a practical resource for you in preparation for your journey. In my dream, every entrepreneur has a fighting chance at success.

What the Book is NOT

GET INSPIRED is not a "how to" book. In other words, the book does not provide a step-by-step guide or blueprint to follow for you to discover your passion, your purpose, or your goal. That is the function of the GET INSPIRED course that I offer, which is included in my entrepreneurship program. In the course, startup owners are guided step-by-step to discover their compelling why, to validate their what or business idea, and to make a wish as they set a goal. In other words, the GET INSPIRED course provides a blueprint for HOW to shift your mindset and this GET INSPIRED book is the perfect complement to the course, for a more holistic learning experience.

You can learn more about the course at www.agilebusinessplanning.org/get-inspired or follow me on LinkedIn at https://www.linkedin.com/in/janine-lang-5735a22/

Alex

Ring! Ring! Ring! Pause. Ring! Ring! Ring!

As Alex instinctively reached towards the alarm clock, he glanced out the window to see that it was raining. *Oh great*, he thought to himself. *I think this makes 10 days in a row with no sun.*

7:00 a.m. He scowled as he hit the snooze button.

Realizing that it was Monday morning, Alex pulled the covers over his head. *Just a few more minutes, and then I'll feel like getting out of bed,* he tried to convince himself. *Actually, I might be coming down with something. I have that wrenching feeling in my gut again. Maybe I should just lie here a bit longer and it'll go away.*

But after a few minutes, the feeling didn't go away. Instead, he heard the voice in his head that had been getting louder and louder over the past few months. *I know I'm meant for more. How much longer am I going to stay stuck in this job?*

After slowly dragging his limp body to the bathroom, he stared at his image in the mirror. Trying not to notice the dark circles under his eyes, he reached for his toothbrush.

Perhaps because it was December, Alex found himself reflecting on the past year. He had been working hard on the same project at work for over a year and a half, fixing errors in system code, taking screen shots for training material, and doing other repetitive and boring tasks.

I didn't get an MBA so I could write code, he thought to himself.

Alex's mind drifted to his first day at Dahlia Consulting, one of the biggest consulting firms. He had been recruited to join the firm while he was at Azalea Consulting, a competitor. Alex could remember how hopeful he was at the time. He'd thought he had found a place where he could do meaningful work.

His first year as an information technology consultant was filled with new challenges and variety. The most exciting day for Alex came in his second year, when he was handpicked for a special role on a digital transformation project.

Swishing his toothbrush back and forth, he vividly recalled that deep sense of achievement he felt when the lead partner recognized his outstanding results at the project team's celebratory wrap-up dinner. Standing in front of his applauding peers, he recalled thinking, *this is the kind of strategic work I had always dreamed about doing when I went to MBA school.*

As he looked in the mirror again, he thought to himself, *where's that guy now?*

Since that climactic moment with the firm, everything had gone downhill for Alex. He discovered that implementing a digital transformation strategy isn't sexy or interesting—at least not in his current role. In fact, Alex couldn't recall a single day in the past year and a half when he felt excited to go to work.

Alex's mind was a million miles away as he ran the hairbrush a few times over his head. More specifically, he was thinking back to his final days at Azalea. *This is how I felt when I was ready to move on from my last job...stuck in my career!*

And with that, he left the bathroom without checking his hair. He couldn't bear to look himself in the eye.

The Trigger

Alex was trudging up the sidewalk to the commuter train when he heard the whistle blowing. Out of the corner of his eye, he saw the train roaring into the station and then gradually slowing as it moved up the platform. He knew that he needed to run to catch it, and with a few long strides, he was safely in the door.

During the COVID-19 pandemic, Alex worked from home like most of the population. When the lockdown first occurred, he was skeptical about being able to do his consulting work remotely. However, he quickly settled into a comfortable routine that involved wearing shorts and flip flops every day, every week, and every month year-round.

When his wife Rachel's car broke down for the second time, they decided to see if they could manage with only one car. After all, there was a good transportation system in the city. Everything was turned upside down when Alex's boss announced that staff had to go back into the office three days a week. Alex was hoping that this return-to-work practice would be temporary, but then he noticed how the other partners at the firm had started going into the office regularly. *Ugh!*

When Alex walked into the office on Monday morning, the three project team members who were already there mumbled, "Morning," and kept on working with barely a glance in his direction. To say that morale at Dahlia Consulting had been low lately would be an understatement.

And Alex was no exception. He had been struggling to stay focused on his work lately. His mind was increasingly wandering. He imagined what it would be like to be his own boss...to be able to decide what hours he could work. To be able to decide where to work. Which of course would mean working at home in his shorts and flip flops, every day.

At 11:21 a.m., an email popped into Alex's inbox. When he saw that it was from Janine, a director he worked with last year, he decided to open it right away. He hadn't heard from Janine since she left the firm last year.

Alex had grown accustomed to receiving weekly emails from colleagues announcing their departure from the firm. Turnover in the consulting world was common. Many people leave to go to a competitor or 'cross the street,' as it's often called. But Alex recalled that Janine's farewell was different—she was leaving to start her own business.

Alex's curiosity was piqued. *I wonder how she's doing,* he thought. He opened the email and read it.

Thinking of you. We should catch up for coffee soon. Let me know...

Since she was obviously on her laptop, Alex decided to pick up the phone and call. As he listened to Janine's story, he wanted to be supportive, but he found himself struggling with feelings of excitement and jealousy at the same time as she outlined how her business had grown over the past year. She described all the places on her bucket list that she had traveled to since leaving the firm, like Italy, Portugal, Spain, and France.

That was the tipping point for Alex. He couldn't contain his emotion any longer. "Oh my God! That's my dream job!" he told her.

They made plans to have coffee later that day. Alex wanted to hear the whole story.

Maybe there's a message in there for me about how to get unstuck, he thought to himself.

Part A:
Discovering Your Passion

Lesson 1

Don't Stay Stuck in a Pity Party of 'What You Want to Move Away From'

Alex was running a few minutes late. While Janine waited in front of the coffee shop, she decided to catch up on her email. She pulled her head up just in time to see Alex coming around the corner. Trying to get his attention, she stretched her hand up over the line-up that was forming at Starbucks and waved to him.

"I'm so sorry I'm late, Janine—you know what it's like trying to get out of that place some days."

"Oh—don't worry about it. And yes, I certainly know about the long hours. I don't miss those days."

Alex looked like he was forcing himself to smile. "Congratulations again on your decision, Janine. Although I have to admit that selfishly, I've really missed you at the firm."

They both walked inside the coffee shop where they ordered lattes and managed to find two seats together. Eventually the conversation turned to work.

"Mid-year promotions are coming up. Is your name on the promotion list?"

He shook his head. "No, I'm being passed over for promotion. I thought that after three and a half years as a senior manager with the firm, I would've been considered for a partner position by now."

"Sorry to hear that. I know you've worked hard for it, and I can see you're disappointed."

He nodded. "The good news is I think management believes that I'm ready, but as you know, there needs to be a position available. Since there are so few partners in our practice, I'm not sure I can expect to advance for the next few years."

"That must be pretty demotivating."

"Thanks, I appreciate that. To be honest, I'm not sure I'll want to stick around that long. I'm not finding the work very challenging these days. And by not challenging, I mean that I'm bored out of my mind. And by these days, I mean for well over a year now."

Janine sat up straighter in her chair. "Really? I'm surprised to hear you say that. The last time we spoke, you told me you loved the digital transformation work you were doing. You sounded so excited!"

"That was the strategy phase, and it was so awesome! The work was exciting, challenging, and fun. I really enjoyed the regular meetings with the CEO where we got to help him create his digital strategy for the whole company."

"Boy! That's amazing experience you're getting."

Alex lowered his head. "Yes, it WAS. Now that the project is in the implementation phase, the work is completely different. Can you believe that I'm actually writing code? I'm literally taking screen shots of the new technology for training manuals. I had no idea how monotonous the work would be."

"I hear ya. So, are you thinking of quitting?"

Alex grinned. "I would be lying if I didn't admit that I've been thinking about it. On those days when I don't have to turn on my brain to do my job, there's a voice in my head saying, '*Alex, you're meant for more.*'"

"That sounds familiar!"

"Tell me your story. When did you know that it was time to move on?"

Janine sat back in her chair and thought for a moment. "I reached a point where I didn't feel like I was learning any more. After so many years in the same consulting role, I had reached the point where I wasn't growing. I didn't feel like the new projects were stretching me or building my skills."

Alex chuckled. "So, you stopped having to turn your brain on to go to work too?"

Janine smiled. "That's a good description, but I think an even bigger motivator for me was compensation. Last year, I had the best year of my career. I sold over $5 million in consulting projects for the firm—a milestone for me."

Alex's eyes grew large. "Wow, that was a terrific year for you!"

"Yes, and it certainly earned me a rating of outstanding. So you can imagine how disappointed I was when I received a salary freeze. It didn't matter that I was the top earner in sales AND top contributor for billings in the practice. I was already earning above the mid-point in the salary range, so no salary increases. No discussion. Period."

"I can't believe that! You didn't get anything for bringing in millions of dollars for the firm?"

"To be fair, yes, I did receive something. The accounting executives upstairs thought that a $500 Sonos speaker would be an appropriate reward for my role in winning a $3 million piece of new business."

Alex laughed out loud. "Hmm. I'm no accountant, but that does seem like a pretty good ROI—for the firm, that is. Sorry, I shouldn't be laughing."

Janine was chuckling too. "No, really, it's fine. Actually, It's hysterical. When the executive's assistant contacted me to get my address where she could send the gift, I remember thinking, *'you can just courier the keys to my new car to my home.'* Little did I know what was coming."

"That's too funny!" Alex was roaring.

"Truthfully, I was still hopeful that I would be taken care of at the year-end compensation discussion. Needless to say, I wasn't ready for the salary freeze and the promise of a few extra dollars in bonus. At that moment, I decided that I was worth more than what I was making."

"I get it! So that's when you decided you were ready to leave?"

"Not quite. You see, I know how big companies work and how salary ranges and increases are set. I've been at this a long time. I think the real clincher for me was the lack of flexibility. I reached a point where I wanted to do more traveling, and that didn't seem possible in a full-time corporate position."

"I know what you mean about the lack of flexibility. During the pandemic, I got into a routine of dropping off my stepson Joey at school in the mornings and taking him to basketball practice twice a week after school. But now that my project team is being ordered to go into the office a couple of days a week, it's been a real adjustment on all of us."

"I'm hearing that from all of the colleagues that I've kept in touch with."

"We'd also been able to get rid of one of our cars and were saving a ton of money, but now that I have to start going in again, it's looking like we're going to be vehicle shopping. This back-to-the-office policy is really costing us a lot of money. Not to mention the fact that I need new business clothes, since I put on 10 pounds during the pandemic. The extra weight wasn't that apparent when I was wearing baggy shorts and flip flops every day." Alex pulled on his belt buckle as if to loosen the top of his pants that were tightly fitted around his waist and grinned sheepishly.

Janine laughed again. "Agreed! Working from home was far more comfortable than working in the office."

Alex smiled. "That's one of the big reasons why I've found myself wondering what life would be like if I was running my own business. And then I saw your email pop into my inbox."

Janine looked down, reflecting on the conversation. "So, what I hear you saying is that there are a few reasons why you're thinking about starting a business. From where I sit, they sound like examples of what I think of as 'what you want to move away from.'"

"What do you mean?"

"Well, you've described a few things you're dissatisfied about with your current work situation. Things that you want to move away from in your career, in other words. You started by describing the lack of career advancement—being passed over for promotion. Then there's the lack of meaningful work—you mentioned that the implementation work isn't nearly as interesting or fulfilling as the strategy work you did. Then there's the lack of flexibility—not being able to choose your own hours, where you work and therefore what you wear every day."

"That sums it up pretty well! What a mess. I had such high hopes for my career when I joined the firm. I can't believe what a failure this has turned out to be."

"Alex, I know it's painful to talk about, but the fact that you can articulate what you don't like about your current work situation means that you've taken an important first step forward in your career. Learning from failure is painful but it sets a precedent for moving forward, from my perspective, anyway."

"There are definitely a few more things that I didn't mention, but those are the main reasons."

Janine sat back in her chair. "You might be surprised to hear this, but a lot of people miss that important step. For some people, it's too painful to think about why they hate their work, so they try to ignore it or push it out of their mind, which is even worse."

"Well, I can understand why. After all, it's exhausting dragging myself out of bed and into work every day."

"I've been there. When we feel stuck in a job, we often feel tired, stressed, and even overwhelmed. And over time, it's not unusual to feel helpless to change our situation, which is why it can be difficult to take action to make a change, even though we may be miserable going into work every day."

"As a startup coach, how do you help people with that?"

"Every person is different in terms of how they deal with workplace stressors. I'm not an expert in the wellness area, and I don't want to minimize the impact of disengagement and stress. Some people reach a point where they need professional help to cope with more serious situations. The clients I work with typically just need a little help to turn the corner...you could say I give them a nudge to start channeling their energy into thinking positively about the future."

"Have you worked with clients who were really angry?"

"Sure. For several years, I ran the entrepreneurship program at an outplacement firm that helps downsized professionals to transition to another role. Many were angry about losing their jobs and didn't want to return to corporate positions. They were typically VERY motivated to start a business."

Alex's eyes widened. "Makes sense—I would be too if I lost my job."

"Pain can be a powerful motivator for change. There are lots of examples of professionals who were fired, laid off, or left a toxic work environment—and that pain motivated them to go on to start their own successful companies. A well-known example is Steve Jobs, who was fired from Apple, the company he founded, and went on to start NeXT which he sold for almost half a billion dollars."[7]

Nodding, Alex added, "True. And then there's Michael Bloomberg, who was fired at 39, and the next day started up a knowledge distribution business that nobody at the time said would ever succeed. I read somewhere that

15 years later, he was a billionaire and today he's worth over 100 billion dollars."[8]

"That's another great example. We didn't have to look hard to identify very successful entrepreneurs who used their pain as motivation. In every case, when one door closed, another one opened. And until that door opens and the silver lining becomes apparent, it can be helpful to use that pain as a motivator. But I wouldn't suggest it as a long-term strategy for success. Hanging onto bitterness and revenge isn't healthy."

"Agreed. That makes perfect sense."

Janine paused a moment to reflect on the discussion before continuing. "Alex, I'm not sure about your silver lining."

"What do you mean?"

"I'm fairly clear about what you want to move away from or what's keeping you stuck in a job you hate right now. But I'm not sure you've mentioned why you want to start a business. Or perhaps I just missed it?"

"You know, I really want to do what you're doing. I've always pictured myself starting my own business, like my father did when he was about my age. I know I'd be happier following in my father's footsteps and running my own strategy consulting business."

"I see. How do you believe your life would be different as a business owner?"

Lesson 1 Summary

Key Takeaways:

The most common sources of disengagement that employees want to 'move away from' are:

- A lack of opportunities for career advancement
- A lack of meaningful work
- No opportunity to learn or to grow
- Compensation not keeping up with living expenses
- Lack of flexibility

Question to Consider:

What are all the things that you want to move away from in your current work environment?

Lesson 2

Don't Expect to Figure Out Overnight 'What You Want to Move Toward'

Alex lowered his head, deep in thought. "I suppose my life as an owner would be the opposite of what I described. Or maybe, it's the life I enjoyed during the pandemic where I had more flexibility and wore flip flops every day."

Janine smiled, "Maybe. Although I doubt that wearing flip flops is the secret to your job satisfaction."

Alex laughed. "Agreed. It's up there, but it's definitely not at the very top of my list. Umm...well."

Janine jumped in when she saw Alex was struggling. "Listen—that's a common reaction. In my experience with coaching startups for over two decades, most people can tell you what they DON'T want in their careers. But most people have difficulty describing what they DO want."

"That's a relief. But I'm a bit surprised."

"You shouldn't be. We often wrongly assume that it'll be obvious what's important to us in our careers, once we've figured out what we don't like. Sure—it might give you some hints...like flexibility to be able to work where you want. And yes, to be able to wear what you want. But that doesn't necessarily clarify what's MOST important to you—does it?"

Alex chuckled, "I guess you're right. Footwear doesn't seem like criteria I should be using to decide on my next career choice." They both laughed.

"Listen, Alex, I'm teasing you a bit about the flip flops, but the reality is most people enjoyed the dress code associated with remote working. And the reason we're talking about it is because casual attire is one of the many benefits of working from home. Right?"

Alex sat up in his chair. "Yes. I've never been a morning person, so being able to set my own hours and work when I'm most productive was awesome. And being able to take care of errands during the day when stores are less busy actually made them enjoyable to do, and working out at the gym during off peak hours, and taking Joey to basketball practice, and, and, and...I could go on and on."

"I get it. As you're saying, there are lots of benefits that you would enjoy if you decided to start your own business—many of those related to flexibility. That's one of the reasons why it can be difficult to understand what the real driver is for wanting to start a business."

Alex thought for a second. "Maybe that means that flexibility is most important to me."

"Yes, I'm hearing that's important to you. As a result, it's easy for you to brainstorm lots of benefits. In order to discover your compelling why, we want to unpack those benefits and see what's really behind them, that's driving you towards entrepreneurship."

"I'm not sure I'm following."

"What if flexibility was a means to an end, rather than the end itself? Let me share my own example to explain. When I decided to start my first business over 20 years ago, I thought that control over my career was most important to me. After all, I had just been downsized after nine years in my very first job. I was devastated!"

"Understandable—I'm sorry to hear that, Janine."

"Thank you. What's interesting is that the business I started was very profitable. I made more money in that first year than I was making in my full-time job the previous year, but I was constantly stressed about money."

"What! Why is that?"

"Because as an entrepreneur, the money was 'lumpy.' I was confident in my ability to sell but I wasn't sure when the projects would land, and I only got paid after I finished delivering a training program. What I learned from that experience is that I have a high security need, and when I didn't have a regular paycheck coming in, I was stressed about paying the bills."

"That makes perfect sense. As an entrepreneur, you really didn't have control over the timing of your income."

"Exactly! And if I had taken the time to unpack why control over my career was important to me, I would have realized that I wanted the business because it provided the means to achieve our goal of buying the lake house we wanted. For me, it was about having a deeper connection with the friends and family that we would entertain there. But what I didn't stop to realize was that I would have less control over the timing of my income, which was pretty important since my ex-husband and I had just bought our dream home in the country and increased the size of our mortgage."

"Ah—it sounds like you've learned a lot about yourself from the experience!"

"I really did. And one of the learnings is that when our reason for starting a business is linked to a need or strong desire that we have, then it's more likely to be compelling. In this case, it was wanting to spend more time with my family and friends."

"So you're suggesting that if I dig deeper into why flexibility is important to me, I might realize that my connection with Joey is the real reason why I want a business?"

Janine chuckled. "It's possible, although everyone's reasons are personal, so you'll need to decide that for yourself."

"Well, when I think about the time that I spent shuttling Joey back and forth to school, I really enjoyed that one-on-one time with him. Now that he's older, he spends more time with his friends and isn't home as much. That was my guaranteed time to connect with him every week...you know, to catch up on what was going on with him."

"Ah. Sounds like connection IS important to you."

"Well, he's growing up so fast. If I don't spend that time with him now, I don't see it happening when he's older."

"I get it. Your connection with Joey is important to you, not to mention the fact that you've attached some urgency around experiencing that now, before it's too late."

"That totally resonates!"

Janine smiled. "I'm glad. But before you decide that's it—that's what is driving you forward, I'd like to share another reason why it can be challenging to identify your compelling why, or what you're moving toward. You see, in addition to all those great benefits, there can also be some negative impacts or unintended consequences."

Alex squinted. "How so?"

"When I shared my example with you earlier, I mentioned that I wasn't prepared for the downside of less control over the timing of the money coming in, even though my total income for the year was higher than before. And when my need for a regular paycheck wasn't being met, I shut down the business. In other words, it can be challenging when some needs are being met but not others."

Alex nodded. "That's a great point. I'll need to do some thinking about the implications. When I mentioned the idea of starting a business to Rachel last week, her initial reaction was to be supportive because she knows I would love to do more strategy work. But since we're talking about buying another car, I guess we'll need to talk about the unintended consequences, like the financial impact of starting a business. I might not have any money coming in at all when I'm just starting out."

"100 percent! And I'm curious; what is it about strategy work that you find so exciting? I get that the digital implementation stuff you've been doing is boring."

"Oh! I love feeling that I'm making a difference to my clients—that I'm impacting their business. And the strategy work does that for me."

"Terrific!"

"Wait—I'm confused now! Are we saying that connecting with Joey is most important or having an impact on my clients?"

Laughing, Janine responded, "Great question. Like I said earlier, it can be difficult to figure out our compelling why—the real reason we're driven to start a business. As you're seeing, we often have two reasons—or even more than two, that can seem almost equally compelling. Yes—we were just talking about your desire for a greater connection with Joey as your compelling why. And now we're saying that the opportunity to do meaningful work might be the real driver."

"Great. So, how do I choose?"

"Some coaches will tell you that you need to pick just one compelling reason for starting a business, but I'm not one of those coaches. You can be motivated by both connection and making a difference. You may even notice that their relative importance changes over time. For example, you might find that for the next six months, your connection with Joey is more motivating while you're driving him to school. Or even for the next two years, until he moves away to university. The point is that you don't have to decide what is a compelling why for the rest of your life. What's important is what's compelling for you right now."

"Ah—that's a relief. I was feeling pressure to understand what would be motivating for me one month, one year or ten years down the road."

"That's a common myth that exists—some people believe that your 'why' is not supposed to change over time. But that's just not realistic."

Alex nodded in agreement. "So, how do you know when you need a new why?"

Janine leaned back in her chair. "To answer that, let's first look at the purpose that is served by knowing your why."

"Oh good. I was wondering about that myself earlier."

"I tell my startup clients that there are three main reasons for knowing your why. The first is that it's typically the catalyst for creating the business, by setting you in **motion**. Most people think about starting a business for a while, and their 'compelling why' is often the reason that compels the person to actually follow through on starting it up."

Alex recalled how he struggled to get out of bed that morning. "So, that voice that keeps telling me I'm meant for more will start asking me when am I going to start a strategy consulting business."

Janine chuckled. "You could say that! Yes, that inner voice, or the self-talk, can give you the kick you need to get going. The second reason is that it provides **momentum** for the journey, so that you stay in motion. I'm sure you know that you are about to embark on a learning journey, where not every strategy that you try will work. In other words, staying focused on the big picture by remembering why you're doing this can be invaluable for staying positive, while you're figuring out what works and what doesn't work in those early days and establishing your success routine."

"You're right—I've certainly heard about the emotional roller coaster ride when you're on an entrepreneurial journey."

"On that point, let me share with you a little hack that I tell my clients, something that's worked for me since starting this second business. Once you identify your compelling why, either write it down or take a picture of it and then put it somewhere that you'll look at regularly. Think of it as giving that voice in your head the exact words that you'll need to hear, as a reminder to keep going."

"I love that!"

Janine leaned forward. "In your case, you'll want to have pictures or descriptions of BOTH of your whys, and you'll use them at different times, right? The only downside of having multiple whys is that if you're confused about what's important to you at a particular point in time, you might lose the clarity you need to drive you forward. Does that resonate—having a clear vision of your why at any point in time?"

"Yes, absolutely. What's the third reason?"

"It's closely related to the second one—**maintain the commitment**. When you're riding those ups and downs, there are days when you'll be tempted to want to get off, like I did with the first business. The reality is that many businesses fail because the business owner gives up. Reminding yourself of your compelling why can be the difference between sticking it out and giving up."

"I get it. If I'm passionate about the cause, I guess it can help with that inner voice we're talking about."

Janine shook her head. "You sound like me before I started my first business. I used to think that the emotional side of the business was fluff, and I just needed to have a sound business idea, develop a clear roadmap, and then make it happen. After all, I was driven and self-disciplined."

Alex leaned in. "Yeah—go on."

"I learned the hard way that without a compelling reason, I wasn't really committed enough to building it. So, when things got tough, it was a real test of that commitment. If a business is something that you're just kinda interested in doing, you'll give up before it's successful. But if you're serious about the business, you've at least got a chance."

Janine paused for a moment to let it sink it, and then asked, "So, are you just INTERESTED in starting a business, or are you SERIOUS about it?"

"Wow—that's a powerful question. It's time to look in the mirror. If the business is something that I'm just going to dabble with for a while and see how it goes, I suppose I shouldn't waste my time."

"Exactly. You're either ready to go all in or you're not. And if you decide to go all in, then I think you still have some work to do on your 'compelling why' before you're ready to start up that business."

"Oh? I thought we figured that out. What's the work?"

"Today, I gave you a bit of a taste test by asking you a couple of questions. In my courses, I go much deeper and take my clients through a series of activities to help them to discover their passion."

"I see. I'd be interested in learning more. I don't think I remember taking any courses on that, even in business school."

"You probably didn't. I didn't learn this in the entrepreneurial courses I took in university. Our school system doesn't do a good job of preparing people to be entrepreneurs. That's why most people don't know what the work actually is."

"That's unfortunate. It means that most people probably don't know how to get unstuck from a bad work situation."

"That's true, Alex. And even when I tell some people what the work is, they're not prepared to do it. That's what separates the people who are dabbling from the people who are serious."

"Is it easy for you to recognize whether your client is a dabbler or serious?"

"Yes—I just listen. The ones who dabble are typically still stuck in the past—they talk about what they want to move away from. The ones who are serious about getting unstuck in their careers talk about what they want to move toward."

Lesson 2 Summary

Key Takeaways:

The most common sources of motivation that employees want to 'move toward' are:

- Greater flexibility, in terms of when they work, where they work, and what they wear while working
- Better balance of work and life demands
- Greater control over finances
- Deeper connection with loved ones
- Making a difference or having an impact
- The main benefits of 'knowing your why' are:
- Motion: Serves as a catalyst for taking action
- Momentum: Helps to build maintain optimism during the low points of the journey
- Maintain the Commitment: Increases the likelihood of 'sticking with it,' when you feel like quitting
- Your passion or compelling why will evolve over time as your life situation and your needs change.

Question to Consider:

What are all the reasons why you are moving toward starting a business?

Lesson 3

Don't Overlook the Power of 'Wanting to Move Others'

J anine stared at Alex for a few seconds, trying to imagine whether he could relate to being a dabbler or serious. She realized that she likely made it sound too black and white. "Before we leave this topic of passion, I'd like to share with you a mistake that I made when I first started this second business. You see, I felt serious about starting a business but there were times that I felt like a dabbler in that first year. I realized later that the reason for my dabbling wasn't a lack of commitment—the issue was that my 'why' wasn't very compelling."

"That'd be really helpful to hear your story."

Janine smiled. "Okay—I'll share the lesson that I had to learn the hard way. Like you, one of the aspects that attracted me to starting my own business was the flexibility that I would have to set my own schedule. However, for me, flexibility meant more time for travel. In fact, that's one of the reasons I told my boss I wanted to quit my full-time job, and I booked a trip to Europe right away—my plan was to celebrate my departure from the firm."

"Exciting! You've always talked about going to Europe!"

"Yes, I was finally going to tackle my bucket list of travel destinations. The only problem with that was once I returned from my trip and started the business, I didn't book a vacation in that first year. So the first lesson that I learned was that I was a terrible boss—not giving myself any time off!"

Alex laughed. "I do recall you taking at least two weeks off every year, so I can see why you might have surprised yourself that you had NO time off when you became your own boss!"

"True—that was a wake-up call at the end of the year when I had to admit that I had failed miserably on my travel goal." They both laughed.

"All kidding aside, I learned an important lesson about taking time to reflect and identify what I didn't like about my previous work environment, with a goal of making sure that I was designing the ideal work environment that I wanted. So the first correction I made was to be more specific about my ideal travel schedule—in what months and for how long. The answer was six weeks! Two weeks in Europe in the spring, another two weeks in Europe in the fall and another two weeks in the winter—usually to go somewhere warm."

"That's why you suggested to me that I write down what I want to move away from?"

"Yes, exactly! The second lesson I learned when I changed my 'why' from wanting more flexibility for travel to wanting more flexibility for travel WITH loved ones. That's when I really got excited."

Alex shrugged. "What's the difference?"

Janine sat back in her chair. "We do more for others than we do for ourselves! It's human nature. So, when one of my reasons for starting a business involved the impact it could have on my friends and family who I could take with me on my travels, that's when I got really fired up."

"Ah—I see now."

When she saw Alex nodding, she continued. "I can either visualize my bucket list being checked off, or I can picture myself in Europe attending a cooking school with my girlfriends drinking wine and laughing. Which of those two 'whys' sounds more compelling?"

Alex raised his eyebrows. "I see what you mean. I want to be cooking and drinking wine!"

"Exactly! So, tell me which of the two options that you're considering involves doing more for others?"

Alex looked down. "Let me think. When I reflect on what it would mean to spend quality time with Joey, what goes through my mind is that I hear him opening up and telling me what's going on with his life. Because we have a good bond, he often asks me for advice on topics that he doesn't always feel comfortable discussing with his mom. When I see that smile and confident look on his face, that lights me up!"

Janine clapped with excitement. "That's awesome. Knowing that you're helping Joey grow into a more confident young man must be tremendously satisfying. There's a lot of research that suggests that altruistic acts of kindness to others naturally make us feel happy. It's evident that seeing Joey happy and confident gives you a tremendous sense of pleasure."

"No question! And like we said, I'm feeling a sense of urgency around that opportunity to make an impact on Joey."

"That's an important consideration—good work! Now for your second option. What impact would it have if you were doing meaningful work?"

Alex looked like he was struggling a bit to describe his feelings. "I know I said that I'm driven to do more strategic work because it'll help my clients, but if I'm holding up a mirror, I would have to admit that there are far more benefits to me from doing that kind of work. It would be more challenging and rewarding, and I've always wanted to be considered a respected advisor to executives. The sense of accomplishment would be huge!" Alex paused. "I do hear myself. When I'm being honest, this feels more like what I would be doing for myself than for my clients."

Janine winked. "You get an A plus for self-awareness! To be fair, I know you'll do great and that your clients would benefit greatly—especially since you've gained more and more experience in this area. But this motivator does sound more intrinsic."

Alex reached over his shoulder as if to pat himself on his back. "It might look like I'm taking the credit for landing on the right answer, but thank you for the coaching to help me to see that my motivation comes from the connection with Joey."

Janine laughed. "Truthfully Alex, I think it was Maslow who was doing the coaching here."

Alex looked around as if to be looking for someone else, then understanding lit up his face. "Do you mean the Maslow who created the hierarchy of needs?"

Janine nodded. "That's exactly who I mean. I didn't mention Maslow earlier when we were talking about needs, because I wanted to understand first why flexibility is important to you...and what aspects of the work environment are important to you. You needed to discover first that flexibility is about connection to Joey for you, and you needed to discover that doing strategy work is about your sense of accomplishment. Now that you've uncovered WHY you're passionate about each of those two options, Maslow's hierarchy of needs can be used to gain insights as to why we might place greater importance on connection over accomplishment."

"Do you use Maslow's hierarchy of needs in your coaching to help people to choose one over another?"

"No, I don't think Maslow's hierarchy should be used as a decision-making framework. I do however think it can provide a perspective on human behavior in general, and how a set of needs or human drives motivate us. However, my point of view is that motivation is not a science. People are highly complex and can be motivated to act for lots of reasons. Basic human drives are only one perspective."

"Makes sense. Didn't Maslow say that we do more for others than ourselves?"

"Good question. I don't know if that phrase has ever been attributed to anyone. But if you recall Maslow's five levels of needs, you might think that he would have uttered that sentiment."

Alex looked away. "To be honest, I'm not sure I remember the levels. We studied the hierarchy in a psychology class I took, but that feels like a hundred years ago."

Janine chuckled. "Well, here's a quick refresher. According to Maslow, Level 1 needs are physiological ones—basic survival needs like food and water and Level 2 needs are related to safety—physical, but also emotional and financial.[9] Thinking back to my example, you can probably see more clearly now why I decided to exit the business when my need for a steady paycheck wasn't being met. I see many startup owners reluctant to leave their jobs because they're uncertain if their financial security needs will be met. That fear of financial instability holds many people back from following through on their entrepreneurial dreams."

"I can see why. How do your clients overcome that?"

"When my clients are looking for the confidence that their financial needs will be met—that they'll have enough money coming in to make ends meet—I give them the assurance that my business planning course contains a section on financial planning. I believe every startup owner needs to spend some time focusing on the cash flow of their business—examining the earning potential of their business idea. Armed with that knowledge, we talk about different options they have for supplementing the revenue from their business, so they can make ends meet. Boy—I wish somebody had given me that gift before I started my first business."

"I can see how finances would be a deal breaker for a lot of people. As much as I hate my job, I need that peace of mind that Rachel, Joey, and I will be okay if I decide to start a business."

"For sure. So, once we know that those basic needs aren't at risk, we can move on to the next level of needs. These higher-level needs will be more relevant to you. You'll recall that Level 3 needs are social—which is about love, connection, and belonging."[10]

"Ah—so connection with Joey is a Level 3 need?"

"That's right. Level 4 needs are self-esteem—feelings of accomplishment, respect, and independence, for example."[11]

"I see. So meaningful or challenging work would be an example of a Level 4 self-esteem need?"

"I'm not an expert at the framework, but I think Maslow would agree with you." Janine shrugged.

"Thanks for the reminder about the levels. Does Maslow believe that our Level 3 connection needs should be met before our Level 4 self-esteem needs?"

"Again, I'm not an expert, but popular belief is no, we can be motivated by different needs that are at multiple levels. Generally, as we grow, we tend to be motivated by higher-level needs. It's not a science, however, and everyone is different in terms of their beliefs, values, and experiences that influence their behavior."

"I hear you. You're reminding me again not to rely on Maslow to decide about my why."

"You're right, and now to finish the framework, Level 5 is self-actualization—realizing your potential or feelings of self-fulfillment."[12]

"That's right! It's coming back to me now."

"Great! I'm glad that was helpful. I see Maslow's framework as a way of categorizing or thinking about your various needs, which can be helpful to make sense of all our emotions that pull us in different directions. We can use Maslow's framework to at least attach a name to those needs and desires, which can enhance our self-awareness of them."

"You've definitely given me something to think about, Janine."

"That's awesome! The work that my clients do to discover their why or their passion involves building self-awareness. Rather than focusing on the pain, the idea is to focus on the pleasure you would get from starting a business, or whatever it is moving you toward entrepreneurship. Human nature demonstrates that it's easier to identify the pain. Figuring out what makes us happy is harder."

Alex shook his head. "That's ironic—it seems so backwards."

Janine grinned. "So true!"

Alex shifted the conversation back to an earlier point. "Actually—I DO know the answer. Doing digital strategy work makes me happy. There—I've figured it out!"

Lesson 3 Summary

Key Takeaways:
When we have an emotional connection to our 'compelling why,' we will be that much more committed to it.

Maslow's hierarchy of needs can be a useful framework for providing self-awareness or insights into the different categories of needs:

- Level 1: Physiological. Food, water, or other basic survival elements
- Level 2: Safety. Physical, emotional, and financial
- Level 3: Social. Love, connection, and belonging
- Level 4: Self-esteem. Accomplishment, respect, and independence
- Level 5: Self-actualization. Realizing your potential or feelings of self-fulfillment

Although we are motivated by both pain and pleasure, most people are able to more easily identify the source of their pain than identify what brings them pleasure.

Question to Consider:
What are all the needs that are influencing your desire to start a business?

Part B:
Discovering Your Purpose

Lesson 4

Don't Confuse Passion and Purpose

J anine leaned forward in her chair. "Yes—you mentioned that you're excited about doing strategy work. That means that you're likely clear about your purpose, which is different from your passion."

Alex had a confused look on his face. "Oh? I would have used the terms interchangeably."

Smiling, Janine realized that she needed to do some coaching. "That's common—many people confuse passion and purpose. And to be honest, I've heard some coaches use the terms interchangeably, so it's understandable that people can be confused. I've heard many conflicting definitions over the years. Let me share mine."

"That'd be great. Frankly, I would have said that they're the same thing."

"In a nutshell, I use the term **passion** to refer to your 'why,' and I use the term **purpose** to refer to your 'what.'"

"Okay." Alex sat up attentively.

"Let me explain. We've just been talking about your passion—your motivation for wanting your own business. Your passion refers to **why** you want to start it. **Why** you will stay committed to building that business, even when things get tough. **Why** your business MUST succeed! The reason why it's important to discover your compelling why is to find within you the motivation to stick it out and to be successful."

"So, my passion is my why—why I'm passionate or feel strongly about this career path?"

"Well said! That's why we spent so much time talking about your needs and desires, with some good coaching from Maslow and his hierarchy of needs. The intent was to help you to recognize what the most powerful source of motivation or compelling why is for you."

"Okay, that makes sense."

In a jesting tone, she asked, "Do you remember the three reasons why I suggested it's important that you're clear about your why?"

"Umm ... three?"

"I'm just teasing you...it's not a test. I just wanted you to have a quick reminder before we shift gears and start talking about purpose."

"Okay—I think you said something about motion."

"That's right! The first reason is a compelling why can set you in **motion,** when you're feeling stuck in your career. The second reason is it can help you with

momentum, reminding you that you're building the business to help others that you care about, and not only yourself. And the third reason is to **maintain** or more accurately **sustain** the business when you have the moments of self-doubt or fear and want to quit. I use those three words that start with M—motion, momentum, and maintain, as my reminder."

Alex thought for a second. "Isn't there a fourth M in there—money?" He laughed.

Janine smiled. "I suppose there's a link between knowing your why and business success or money. Many high-performance coaches will tell you that empirical evidence can be found that links knowing your why to a shift in your mindset. It's a fact, and not my opinion, that knowing your why can help you build your resilience, which is arguably the most important attribute of a successful entrepreneur."[13]

"Okay—so now we have five M's if you include mindset. I didn't realize that there's science behind the compelling why or passion."

Janine laughed. "The truth is that I could quote research to you all day long, but it won't resonate until you experience first-hand the feeling you get from knowing your why. That's human nature. Alex, do you recall how you felt when I asked you if you were SERIOUS about starting a business or just INTERESTED?"

Alex recalled how Janine's question triggered something in him. "Yeah, I was a bit defensive. That voice in my head was saying, 'Hey—I'm not dabbling with this business idea. I'm going to DO something about it. You'll see!'"

"That's awesome! That inner strength that you felt is science. That fight or spirit in you is science. I'm not a medical doctor, so I can't tell you what happens inside of you in physiological terms, but I can tell you that means that starting a business is a MUST DO, and not a NICE TO DO activity, for you. If you didn't have that conviction in you at this stage, I might be worried."

"Ah—that's a good test. Is it always so apparent?"

Janine shook her head. "That's a great question. 'No' is the short answer, because even when we're committed to something, we can still feel uncertain at times. After all, if you've never started a business before, you'll have tons of questions and feel uncertain...truthfully, a lot of the time. Knowing your why doesn't mean that you won't be scared; after all, fear is a common reaction. But knowing your why means that when you notice the fear, you'll remember your compelling why, and you'll do it anyway. That's the difference that knowing your why can make."

Alex looked down. "But what if It's not just fear? What if it's a fact? I mean—I really don't know what I'm doing."

Janine reached out and placed her hand on top of his. "Alex, when you figure out your why, you'll have the motivation you need to figure out the how."

Alex smiled. "Thank you for that. Okay I'm getting my head around passion—what it is and why I need to do more work to discover it. So, how is my passion different from my purpose?"

Janine clapped her hands with excitement. "That's great that you're clear about your passion now. As a reminder, your purpose is your **what**. One definition I like is, 'What do you love to do,' or 'What work makes you feel alive?'

Alex grinned from ear to ear. "I totally loved doing the digital strategy work. However, I do realize that I've only done one project. Can I really call digital strategy my purpose in life if I've only done it once? What if it turns out that I'm not really that good at it?"

"Great question! First, you need to cut yourself some slack. NOBODY is great at something the first time they do it. Or realistically, the first few times. Only through repetition do we master something."

Alex shrugged. "Okay, that's fair."

"Think about when Joey first learned to play basketball. You probably saw him miss lots of shots at the beginning before he started to develop some skills."

Alex nodded. "Sure."

"After doing something once, the only thing we have is enjoyment or excitement when we tried that activity for the first time. What I mean is that if Joey didn't have fun on that first occasion that he played basketball, then he wouldn't want to go back and do it again. And then the more he went, the better he got. And the better he got, the more he wanted to continue."

"That sounds right! I can't believe how he'll jump out of bed at five thirty in the morning to go to basketball practice, but I can't drag him out of bed at ten o'clock on a Saturday to help me cut the grass."

Janine laughed. "Really—that surprises you? All kidding aside, that energy to leap out of bed in the morning when it doesn't come naturally to us is a great example of the power of motivation. Now, you raised a great point earlier about ability. Whether he has any natural talent at it will determine how far he goes. In other words, if he has a dream to play professional basketball, that will be determined by how good he is. But I can guarantee you that no one ever made it into the NBA if they weren't 110% committed to being a professional basketball player and willing to consistently put in the work. To go all in!"

"So true!"

"So, back to your comment about not knowing whether you're good at digital strategy work. The only way you're going to find out if you're good at it is by doing it again and again. You just need to figure out how to do more of it and consistently put in the work to get better at it."

"Do you really think it's just a matter of time and practice?"

Janine smiled. "I believe that we're capable of so much more than we think. We just have to consistently show up every day and do the work. But like professional basketball, you might discover that there are limitations to what you can accomplish with digital strategy work. Over time, you'll figure out whether you can be successful in that business—by your own definition, of course. USUALLY, we're our own worst critic and our mindset is what's holding us back."

Alex cringed. "Okay, that last comment hit home. I've definitely been guilty of being a bit of a perfectionist and holding myself to some pretty high standards."

Janine leaned forward in her chair. "Alex, we only lose when we give up. If you let perfectionism get in the way, you won't have the courage to show up imperfectly, which means you're never going to improve. Knowing you, you'll rehearse a presentation again and again in private before showing up to a meeting with an executive. But you'll need to be okay with the fact that you're never going to be as prepared as you'd like, and it's okay to be a bit 'messy.'"

"I suppose you're right, but when I see the partners in our practice who have been advising executives for decades, it's easy to lose confidence."

Janine shook her head. "Oh, Alex. Don't fall into that trap of comparing yourself to others—especially when you're in the early stages of that learning curve. I see it often. With social media, we see others who are doing similar work, and they appear so accomplished and so confident. I understand the temptation to do it, but I really hope you resist that urge to compare yourself to others, because it's not fair to compare this version of you to a partner, who has been coaching executives for how long?"

"Mark has been a partner for a couple of decades."

Janine smiled. "Try to remember that once upon a time, Mark was in your shoes. Everyone who got great at basketball picked up a basketball one day, for the first time. And everyone who got great at advising executives about their strategy once finished their very first strategy project."

Alex nodded. "That's a great perspective to keep in mind. It's easy to forget that when I see people who make it look easy."

Janine reached over and grabbed Alex's arms and gently shook him. "Alex, you're smart and driven. I've seen you learn about project management when you were determined to become the strongest project manager on your team. And when you studied and practiced, you got good quickly! You eventually became our strongest project manager! I believe you can be great at digital strategy work if you apply that same discipline to that goal. And now you also need to BELIEVE you can."

Alex laughed and relaxed again in his chair, and Janine thought she saw a tear welling up in his right eye. "That means a lot to me. I needed that reminder about what I can be capable of. It's just that it seems like a lofty goal to be a trusted advisor to executives of their digital strategy."

"I understand. Be patient with yourself—you won't get there tomorrow. But if you develop a plan for achieving your goal and consistently follow through on it, you can eventually get there."

Alex smiled. "You sound like Rachel. She always says you can do anything you make up your mind to do. So, just make up your mind."

"That Rachel is a smart woman. Often, I see people struggle with making up their mind about their purpose. Then once they've decided on their business idea, the path becomes clearer."

Alex thought about that for a moment. "Hey—now that I'm thinking about it, I also recall feeling similarly excited the first time I made a bookshelf. So how do I know that my purpose in life is to do digital strategy work and not become a carpenter? Okay, I'm kidding a bit, but you know what I mean."

Janine chuckled. "I get that question a lot, actually. Many people struggle with choosing their business idea or their purpose. Some people have a hundred ideas in their head swimming around. Some people have no idea at all—they only know that they want to start a business. And most people, I find, have narrowed down that list of possible ideas to two or maybe three good ones, and they have a tough time picking one."

"Wow! How do they choose one? "

"Let's look at a couple more definitions of purpose for the answer to that question. Rick Warren wrote a book called *The Purpose Driven Life*. He suggests that you look at 'what's in your hand' to discover your purpose. In other words, what are the natural talents or gifts that you have been given?"[14]

"Hmm. I've never heard of the book."

"You should have! It's the best-selling nonfiction hardback in history. Another definition that I like is one I heard from Anthony Trucks, a performance coach and motivational speaker. I've heard him say something like, 'What would be the reason that God said he made you?'[15] Regardless of your personal religious beliefs, I hope you get the idea."

Alex slumped down in his chair. "Yes, yes, I do! But both of those definitions seem to suggest that I need to be good at something."

Janine noticed that Alex seemed deflated, and reminded him, "And how do you get good at something?"

"Okay, Okay. We need to do something more than once. I hear you—you're saying I shouldn't give up on the idea that strategy work could be my thing until I have a little more experience under my belt."

Janine smiled, knowing that Alex got the message. "I couldn't have said it any better!"

"I'm curious though. This might be a silly question, but are we talking about my personal purpose or are we talking about a business purpose? I mean, Rick says 'what's in your hand,' and I personally have a hand. A business doesn't have a hand. Does that make sense?"

Janine chuckled. "Oddly enough—yes, Alex. It makes perfect sense what you're asking. It's actually a brilliant question."

"Hmm. Are you just being nice to me because I looked a little sad earlier?"

They both laughed, and Janine shook her head. "No, I'm not. The concept of purpose applies to a business too. Let's look at some common terms and definitions for the term 'corporate purpose.' You likely remember hearing the terms 'mission' or 'mandate' when you took that business strategy course in university."

"Yes—a mission statement describes what business you're in, or why the business exists."

Janine nodded. "Another A plus! You're absolutely right—that's the definition that we learned in school for a corporate mission statement. Some people use the term mandate instead, but from my perspective, they mean basically the same thing."

"Yes, I've heard that term too. Are there any other terms you've heard over the years?"

"Yes, I'm glad you asked that. Decades ago, when I began facilitating strategic planning sessions with my corporate clients, I learned a definition from Jim Collins that really stuck with me. He's the author of the book *Good to Great*. According to Collins, the truly great companies are aware of their 'Hedgehog Concept'—arguably their purpose or mandate."

"What! Why is it called a hedgehog?"

"Well, according to Collins, they're known to do one thing. They take something complex and organize it into one idea, and everything else is irrelevant. You see, Collins believes that a company's 'hedgehog,' or purpose, has three criteria. One, it's something the company can be best in the world at it; two, it's something they can make money at; and three, it's something they're deeply passionate about."[16]

"Wow—that's cool. Best in the world at? Realistically, I don't think I'll ever be there."

Janine shook her head. "I think the intent is to get you to think about areas where you could have a competitive advantage. It's another way of helping you discover how you'll be able to differentiate your offer from the competition's."

"Oh—that makes sense then. I really like that he suggests I consider the financial aspect of my idea when deciding if it's that's my purpose, or hedgehog." He made air quotes with his fingers around the last word.

"That's great, Alex. I'm glad that resonated. It's important to choose a business idea that you're deeply passionate about, but it's not good enough that you're excited about the idea if it's not a financially viable one. If you can't make money at it then the business isn't going to be profitable, which isn't sustainable."

Alex nodded. "Right! That's why I like that part of the definition."

Janine noticed that Alex seemed concerned. She knew him well enough to know that when his forehead was wrinkled, he was bothered by something. "I thought you liked the hedgehog concept definition. What's up?"

"I do like it! Only now I'm confused. If digital strategy work is my hedgehog concept, is that my personal purpose or my business purpose?"

Janine looked at the empty cup in front of her. "That's a longer discussion. I'm going to need another coffee for that. Can I get you one while I'm up?"

"No thank you. I'll be awake all night."

As she stood up and grabbed her purse, Janine noticed the long line at the counter. She remembered that there was an article on her phone that she had been scanning that morning. "Listen, it looks like I'll be in that line-up for a few minutes. While you're waiting for me, there's an article that you should look at. It's on that very topic." She reached into her purse and grabbed her phone. "Let me find it and send it to you."

"That'd be great—thanks."

Lesson 4 Summary

Key Takeaways:
Common definitions for the term *passion* are:
- Why you want to start a business
- Why you will stay committed to it when things get tough
- Why it must succeed

Common definitions for the term *purpose* are:
- 'What's in your hand' or your natural talents and gifts, according to Rick Warren
- 'What would be the reason that God said he made you,' according to Anthony Trucks
- 'What is your Hedgehog Concept' or 'what can you be best in the world at,' according to Jim Collins

Common terms that are used interchangeably for purpose are mandate, mission, what business you are in, and why the business exists.

Question to Consider:
Which of these terms related to passion and purpose resonate most with you?

Lesson 5

Don't Stay Stuck in a Misalignment of Your Personal and Business Purpose

A lex pulled his phone out of his jacket pocket and found Janine's email at the top of his inbox. He opened it and scanned the title of the article, titled, *The Great Attrition is Making Hiring Harder. Are You Searching the Right Talent Pools?*

His eye scanned the next line. *Hmm. It's written by McKinsey—a reliable source for research*, he thought.

As he scrolled down a bit further, the first statistic jumped out at him. *The share of workers planning to leave their jobs remains unchanged from 2021 at 40 percent.*[17]

He scrolled down to the next page and noticed a chart of global attrition rates. Wondering whether the U.S. would have the highest attrition, his eye was drawn to the biggest number. *Over 60% in India. Wow—that's over half of the workforce, whereas the U.S. has a rate of 40%, exactly the global average.*[18]

He scrolled down a couple of pages where his eye gravitated to a chart entitled *Top reasons for quitting previous job*. His eye scanned the top three: *31% indicated the lack of meaningful work, 36% inadequate compensation, and 41% the lack of career development and advancement as the contributing factors.*[19]

Alex raised his eyebrows at the statistics. *That's interesting,* he thought. *The lack of meaningful work made the list of the top three reasons for leaving—not surprising. My situation isn't that unique after all.*

When Janine arrived back at the table, she noticed that Alex was completely immersed in the article.

"I'm glad that you're enjoying it," she said. "Have you reached the section that describes the five different personas or types of individuals?"

Alex nodded. "I just reached that section and noticed the statistics on reasons for leaving."

Janine pointed to his phone. "You'll want to read the second persona carefully—the author refers to that type as the do-it-yourselfer. I think you'll be able to relate to that one personally," she said with a grin.

Alex gave an inquisitive glance her way.

"Relax, it's not bad. This segment of the workforce is the largest category of employees who quit during the pandemic. It includes the millions who left their corporate positions to start their own businesses in 2020 and 2021. These entrepreneurial individuals tend to be millennials, 25 to 45 years old and motivated by autonomy. They're interested in designing a career for themselves where they can do meaningful work."[20]

Alex sat up. "Oh, that does sound like me! I can't wait to read that section when I get home. But how does the article relate to the question I asked about the difference between personal purpose and business purpose?"

"Aha! Thanks for the reminder. Let me explain. You will read in the article that we all look for a sense of purpose in our work. We like to know that the work we're doing is meaningful."

Alex nodded. "Yes, I noticed that the lack of meaningful work is one of reasons why people quit."

"100 percent! That situation occurs when our personal purpose is not aligned with the business or our employer's purpose. In other words, if we don't believe there is an opportunity to do the kind of meaningful work that we want to do in that workplace, we're more apt to leave."

Alex looked down, and Janine wondered if he was reflecting on whether that described his current situation. "To be fair, the firm would say it's in the business of helping clients to develop and implement their digital strategy," he said. "So I really can't say that my own purpose isn't aligned with the firm's purpose."

Janine was impressed with Alex's critical thinking. "A good observation! If you believe that your purpose is to do digital strategy work, then perhaps they are aligned. Have you considered the possibility that your current project is teaching you what's involved in implementing digital strategy work, which will make you a better advisor when designing your clients' strategies? Think about it for a moment. How likely is it that you could get staffed on another digital strategy project because you've been involved in the full life cycle of a digital project, from strategy phase right through to the end of the implementation phase. From start to finish!"

Alex shrugged his shoulders. "Hmmm. You raise an interesting point."

Janine shook her head. "Don't get me wrong, I'm not telling you what your purpose is. And I'm not telling you to just stick it out. I obviously can't promise you that you'll be staffed on the kinds of digital strategy projects you want to work on. But I do know that the experience I gained implementing an SAP technology solution, from the early stage of creating a business case right through until the last training program was delivered, opened the door for me to many other technology projects."

"That does make sense. I've heard that from other consultants too. I really do appreciate the coaching. It's been hard to see the value of the work I'm doing when I hate going into work every day. That fresh perspective will be helpful."

Janine paused. "I know it's hard to see the big picture sometimes, Alex. As a startup coach, I often work with people who are feeling stuck in their career, like you, because the work they're doing at the time doesn't seem meaningful. Only you can decide whether you're ready for a change in jobs, a change in employers, a change in industry sector, or a change in careers, to entrepreneurship."

Alex looked down. "That's an interesting thought—a change in industry sector!"

"Yes. I've sometimes heard people say they think they might be a better fit in a not-for-profit organization, because their values don't feel aligned with a private sector organization."

"How do you respond to that?"

"When I dig a little deeper to find out what's behind that sentiment, I typically hear frustration about management's focus on the numbers, rather than the people. They don't feel heard or seen at work. For some people, they're hoping that management in a not-for-profit organization will be more motivated by the cause, and not only stakeholder profit. For others, they believe that the nature of the work will be more fulfilling if it's aligned to a cause that they believe in."

"Hmm. I've heard some colleagues say they're passionate about the environment and are looking to do work in that space."

"That's a great example. All I'm saying is that you might simply be in the wrong project, which is temporary, or you might be in the wrong job, which hopefully will be addressed one day through a promotion. You might just be with the wrong company, although you should question whether going to a competitor would provide you with a different experience, unless you're able to join the new firm as a partner. Or you might be in the wrong industry entirely, like the person I just mentioned who is looking to move to the public sector. I'm mentioning all those different possibilities because the article talks about where people are going when they leave."

"So, you're saying that I shouldn't jump to the conclusion that I need to start my own business. There are many different reasons why a person might feel that their individual purpose is not aligned with their employer's purpose."

"That's exactly it. The first step is to be clear about your personal purpose or what work gets you excited. Then it will be easier to figure out what needs to change for you to work in alignment with that purpose. Your job? Employer? Industry? Or your career choice of a corporate vs. an entrepreneurial path?"

"You're right. Those are all possible options, aren't they?"

Janine nodded. "In the article, you'll read about the five types or personas—who they are, reasons why they might quit, and where they might go. You'll see that 35% chose to stay in the same industry, 48% change industries, 18% exit the workforce entirely, and some of them decide to reenter it again, with only 29% returning to a traditional job.[21] And of course, some start businesses."

Alex smiled. "Speaking of re-entering, I've noticed that some people change employers only to return within a year or two."

Janine chuckled. "Well, the grass does look greener on the other side, doesn't it?"

"You can say that again. Every week, I get emails from people who are crossing the street to go to the competition."

Janine smiled. "You mean like me? I've done that more than once in my career. I believe someone once called that the definition of insanity—doing the same thing and expecting a different result." They both laughed, and Janine shook her head. "Honestly, I don't want you to make the same mistake that I did, and that so many other people in our industry make. We don't always take the time to do the work to discover our purpose, and we wrongly assume that the work will be more meaningful in a different company, even when the work is essentially the same. Until we get there, that is. I'm obviously speaking about myself now."

"Aha. That's why I see some colleagues come back within a year or two."

"I was just speaking about my own experience. Everyone is different—it depends why they left in the first place. For some people, the nature of the work is not meaningful or aligned with their personal purpose, as we've been discussing. For others, there's something about the work environment that's not aligned or appealing. For others, they don't believe their boss or their colleagues are supportive."[22]

"Yes, those are some of the reasons I noticed in the article. I heard George left because a competitor offered him a salary increase of fifty thousand dollars."

"Wow, That's a big increase! More commonly, I hear stories about people who leave for an extra ten or twenty thousand a year. I get the temptation, but rarely does a few extra dollars keep them happy for long."

"Yes, it tends to be short-lived. I remember when George left. He said that when his wife heard the competition was offering him an extra fifty thousand a year, he really didn't have a choice."

Lesson 5 Summary

Key Takeaways:
When workers quit, they go to a variety of different landing places:
- 35% stay in the same industry
- 48% change industries
- 18% exit the workforce entirely
- Some of the 'retired and restless' decide to re-enter the working world again, but only 29% return to a traditional job, and some decide to start their own businesses

The largest sector who quit during COVID-19 are millennials between 25 and 45, more likely to be male, who are either self-employed or in part-time, nontraditional, or gig roles.

Question to Consider:
What change(s) are you contemplating? Why?

Lesson 6

Don't Let Anyone Else Tell You What Your Purpose Should Be

J anine shook her head. "Well, you can argue that George didn't have a choice—his wife made it for him. Since I personally fell into this same trap of letting someone else choose my business idea, I obviously understand how this happens. I've often said that when I started my first business, the decision about my business's purpose was given TO me—it wasn't a decision made BY me."

Alex sat up in his chair. "What?"

Laughing at herself, Janine continued. "Let me explain. When I was ready to start a business, someone asked me to deliver a training program. I said yes because I hadn't really decided what my business was going to be about. The thing is, I didn't even really like that work."

"Wow—I'm surprised to hear you say that."

"To be honest, it happens more often than you realize. Many people jump at the first opportunity that lands on their lap, and it may or may not be work they enjoy doing."

"Really? Why do you think that is?"

"There are a lot of reasons why that happens. For starters, if you're known for being a specialist in a particular field and someone in your network learns that you're interested in starting your own business, they may ask you to do a project for them that involves that type of work. They may even think that they're doing you a favor by sending the work your way. After all, if they like you, they may want to help you out when you're just getting started with your business, and it helps them out too because they're looking for someone with that skill set, right?"

"That's true. I hadn't considered that."

"You should! Your network will likely be an important source of potential work if you start your own business. We all want to do business with someone we know and like, so your network will be a real asset."

"Good point!"

"Now here's the tricky part. I've seen people who are clear about their purpose say yes to doing work they hate. One of the reasons we can find ourselves in that situation is that not everyone is comfortable saying no when a friend asks them to do something. We might feel obligated or tell ourselves we'll only make an exception this one time."

"That's what I was thinking I might do if that situation occurs."

"Ah—let's play out that scenario. Let's assume that you say yes, and you do the first strategy implementation project. Naturally your friend is thrilled with your work and therefore asks you to do another technology implementation project."

Alex instantly had a wrenching feeling in his stomach. "Okay, I didn't see that coming! That would be a disaster."

"Exactly! So if you're going to open up Pandora's box and make an exception once, you need to be ready for a client to ask you for a second exception, and then a third. Once the precedent is set, it's harder to say no."

"I can see that—saying yes even once can be a problem."

"Yes, it can be. To be clear though, I'm not telling you to ONLY do work that's aligned to your purpose. I'm just suggesting that if you do take on a project that's outside it, you should manage the expectations of your client—let them know that you appreciate the opportunity and are happy to make this one exception while you're starting up a business that is aligned to a different purpose."

"Is that how you handled the situation?"

Janine sunk down in her chair. "No. Like I said earlier, I had to learn that lesson the hard way. I said yes to that first corporate training program and then one day I woke up wondering, 'How did I get here? When did I decide to run a corporate training business?' Seriously, I wanted to quit. And then I realized, *'That's right—I can't quit. I'm the boss!'* I wanted to fire my clients. Seriously, I've heard similar stories from entrepreneurs, and many shut down their businesses to get out of a bad situation."

"I can see that letting your client dictate what type of business you should start was a tough lesson to learn. You mentioned earlier that this problem is common. Why do you think so many people fall into that trap?"

"Well, when you first establish a business, winning that first job is a BIG DEAL! There might be some financial pressure to make that first sale. So, let's face it—it's tempting!"

"Okay, I must admit that I might be tempted too. My wife and I talked about the fact that I can't expect to earn money from day one, and she's terrific about being patient and supportive, but I can see myself not wanting the business to impact her lifestyle, and certainly not Joey's extracurricular activities."

"That's a natural reaction, Alex—we think about the financial benefits. Another reason is we're confident that we can do the work, right?"

"Sure! If the opportunity that lands on my lap is work that I've done in the past, it's easy. I'll just bang this out quick and move on to the interesting stuff."

"Exactly! It's easy to rationalize that we'll make this one exception while we're waiting for something better to come along. We might not have the focus and the discipline to say that a better use of our time is to proactively go after a better opportunity. After all, most people like to be busy. It makes us feel important, because at least we're doing something productive, and we're making money."

"That makes so much sense. I can hear all the excuses I might have made for saying yes. If that happens to me, I'll try to be self-aware and mindful of the downsides of saying yes."

Janine smiled. "That's great. And if you fall into the trap, at least now I hope you'll recognize it and climb out faster than I did. In other words, fail fast and then get up fast." She laughed.

Alex looked curious. "You've got me thinking. How could I get up fast? Or maybe even avoid failing in the first place?"

Janine sat up in her chair. "There are a few ideas I'd like to share with you. The first piece of advice I always give to clients is when you decide on your purpose or what business you want to be in, a great idea is to ALSO decide what business you DON'T want to be in. In other words, have some clear boundaries in mind."

"Oh—I like that! And as you say, if I decide to overstep that boundary, then shame on me."

At that moment, Janine could practically see the light bulb switching on for Alex. "I just realized. I could say that I'm in the business of doing digital strategy work, but not digital implementation work since that typically involves large teams. That could help me to avoid the pain I'm experiencing right now."

"Yes, I like that your rationale for not being in that business is a benefit for the client. They need a whole team and not only one person for the job. You might want to add something like, 'I appreciate you thinking of me for the opportunity, and I would be happy to refer you to a firm that does those larger implementation projects.'"

"I like that! Oh dear—what if the person actually does ask me for a referral? I'm stuck."

"You could refer them to your current employer, and you could also mention the names of some of your competitors who also deliver those projects."

"That's true. I hadn't considered that the person might not even know which companies do that work, in which case, I would be helping them out. What if they want me to have a role in the project, because they feel comfortable with me, despite the referral? Has that happened to you?"

Janine thought about it for a moment, trying to recall a time when she found herself in that situation. "Come to think of it, I remember a time when a client was so insistent and wouldn't take no for an answer."

"Yes—that's my fear! What did you do?"

Janine had a devilish grin on her face. "Okay—I recall quoting the client a premium price, you might call it. As a business owner, you get to decide how much to charge for your services, so you could always charge a rate that makes it worthwhile for you."

Alex laughed. "I get it! The price would be a deterrent. Oh, but what if they say yes?"

"Great point—when you're deciding on your price, you'll want to ask yourself the question, 'How much would I need to get paid to do that work and feel good about it?'"

"I see. So you would do the work, and have no regrets because you're making a premium wage."

Janine shrugged her shoulders. "Every situation is different. I hope you're getting the idea that there is no one right answer for every situation. As a startup owner, the answer is whatever you decide it will be. I'm just giving you some options to consider in common situations. It's difficult to anticipate how you'll react until you're actually in that very situation."

Alex nodded. "I can see that. If I'm hearing you right, you seem to be suggesting that I need to be a bit flexible about the work I do. Is that right?"

Janine noticed that Alex was fidgeting with his coffee cup. "Yes. Is there something concerning you about that?"

"Well, it's just that I thought the goal was to pursue one purpose—one hedgehog concept. No?"

Lesson 6 Summary

Key Takeaways:
There are several reasons why we might fall into the trap
of letting others decide our business idea or purpose:
- When a loved one or friend asks us to do work that
  we don't like doing, we feel pressured into saying
  yes, regardless of whether their intentions were
  good or not
- We jump at the first opportunity that comes along
- We're desperate to get that first sale under our belt
  when starting up a business
- We rationalize that it will keep us busy until
  something better comes along

Saying yes when asked to do work that we don't like
doing can set a dangerous precedent. Eventually, the
business will feel like something that has been done TO
US, rather than something decided BY US.

Questions to Consider:
Is anyone influencing your decision related to your
purpose?
Are you clear about what business(es) you DON'T want
to be in?

Lesson 7

Don't Fall Into the Trap of Thinking We Have Only One Purpose in Life

"Hmm. Do you recall where you heard that bad advice?" Janine asked.

Alex's eyes widened. "Wow—I'm surprised to hear you say that. Does that mean that some coaches give bad advice?"

"Yes. Some coaches will tell you that we all have one purpose in life, as if it's a cardinal rule of entrepreneurial success. I can tell you many stories of entrepreneurs who have started up many successful businesses—the serial entrepreneur, you might say. "

Alex nodded. "Do you mean they've owned more than one business in their lifetime, or that they own multiple businesses at the same time?"

Janine replied, "Sure! Some sell or exit one business before starting another, but there are lots of entrepreneurs who run multiple businesses at the same time—think of Oprah Winfrey, Elon Musk, Tony Robbins, or Jeff Bezos."[23]

"Ah—true. So why do some coaches believe we should only have one purpose then?"

Janine gave a half smile. "To be fair, let me explain the rationale that I often hear for that argument."

"Okay, that would be helpful."

"Any entrepreneur will tell you how much work is involved in starting up a business, so there's always a risk that you're spreading yourself too thin if you have more than one business that you're starting up. After all, entrepreneurs only get the same 24 hours that employees get in their day."

Alex smiled and jokingly replied, "I'll bet there were days in the beginning when you could have used 30 hours."

Janine laughed. "You've got that right. The other argument is that if you're trying to learn about two businesses at the same time, then you'll come up the learning curve more slowly, and it can easily be overwhelming. That's why many coaches suggest that people spend 100% of their energy on building one business at a time, at least in the early days. Going all in on one business will help you to build the business faster and start earning money sooner. Does that make sense?"

Alex thought about it for a few seconds. "Sure. I see the downside of trying to juggle more than one business, especially in that first year or two."

"The entrepreneurs I just listed have all been running companies for decades. In fact, I'd be willing to bet that most successful serial entrepreneurs started out focusing on one business, and then when it reached a certain size—maybe ten million or a hundred million dollars in revenue—they started adding new products or related businesses. I think that's been the traditional entrepreneurial path, if I can call it that."

Alex nodded. "That does seem like a sound approach. So, why do you sound opposed to it?"

"Don't get me wrong, I'm not against focusing on one business at a time. But there are situations when starting a business is MORE financially feasible if you start with two. That was my strategy."

Alex's eyes widened. "What! You have more than one business? You haven't even been gone a year!" he said loudly.

A few people in the coffee shop turned to look when they heard Alex raise his voice. He noticed the stares and shrank down in his chair. "Oh—sorry. I didn't mean to raise my voice," he said softly, trying to recover from his outburst.

Out of the corner of his eye, he noticed a tall, well-dressed man approach the table. His first reaction was that it was the owner asking them to leave, but the man extended his hand toward Janine, who stood up when she noticed him.

Shaking his hand, Janine greeted him warmly. "It's so great to see you, Mark."

"Nice to see you too. I happened to look over and noticed you sitting here. I hope it's okay that I'm interrupting to say hello."

Janine motioned toward Alex.

"Absolutely—your timing couldn't be better. Mark, I'd like you to meet my friend Alex. We used to work together. Alex, this is Mark. He's an economist and an expert in the gig economy workforce. Isn't that a coincidence?"

After the two men shook hands, Janine invited Mark to join them.

"What does a gig economy workforce expert do?" Alex asked.

Mark lowered his head. "Well, I think Janine is exaggerating by calling me an expert, but my area of focus is identifying workforce trends that are emerging in today's gig economy."

Janine piped up in Mark's defense. "Before I quit my job to start my business, I would call Mark when I was working on an organization design project that required an expert to predict workforce trends—particularly during the pandemic when people started working from home and exiting the workforce in large numbers."

Mark quickly turned to Janine. "So that's why I haven't heard from you recently. Congratulations on starting a business."

Janine nodded. "Yes, I've started a new chapter of my career. In fact, Alex is seriously considering following a similar path. And, coincidentally, we were just talking about the option of a portfolio career."

She turned to Mark to fill him in on the conversation she had been having with Alex. "We were just talking about the advice that some startup coaches give of suggesting that an entrepreneur focus on one business only, and I was about to share my story about why I decided that a portfolio career was an ideal fit. Imagine my surprise when I looked up and there you were—the portfolio career expert."

Mark laughed. "Ah—that explains your comment about the perfect timing. Well, technically Charles Handy is the expert on that trend. At least he's been credited with inventing the concept in his book, *The Empty Raincoat*. Thirty years ago, he predicted that people would work in multiple jobs to meet their financial needs—and that portfolio careers would provide greater flexibility and fulfillment to those people."[24]

Alex was on the edge of his seat. "He predicted that back then?"

Mark chuckled. "He sure did! He was really envisioning what we now call the gig economy. You see, many temporary or contingent workers provide services for multiple organizations. Contingent workers are responsible for 1.7 trillion dollars in revenue globally, according to Staffing Industry Analyst."[25] And it might surprise you to know that over a third of all U.S. workers today are contingent workers, according to Eightfold AI."[26]

Alex leaned forward in his chair. "I didn't realize the trend was that popular."

Mark nodded. "If you're thinking about setting yourself up as a business owner and joining the gig economy, the timing is ideal! The demand for the contingent worker is expected to grow considerably—about 20 to 35 percent per year.[27] Companies are increasingly using temporary workers to handle peak periods, and that's just one trend we're seeing."

"That's right!" Janine exclaimed. "I read somewhere that companies like Intuit, Uber, Lyft, and DoorDash make extensive use of contingent workers for running their day-to-day operations."[28]

"You're right. Those are the companies we read about in the media, but there are obviously many more examples."

Mark turned to face Alex. "Sorry, am I filling your head with too many statistics all at once? I tend to get a little carried away when I'm talking about the future of work."

Alex sat back. "It's great information—really, Mark. It's just a lot to take in at once."

"Let me make this real for you. I think there will be a lot more people wanting to become gig workers than predicted. Think about it; since the pandemic, employees want greater flexibility in terms of where and how they work. That means that employers will have no choice but to turn to contingent workers when they're unable to find people willing to assume traditional full-time jobs. For example, if you assume that 60 percent of an employer's workforce are dedicated employees today, and 40 percent are contingent workers, we may see those percentages reverse themselves in the next 10 to 20 years.[29] At least that's what the case study I read recently said about a global U.K. bank."

"This sounds exciting! I've heard the term contingent worker before, but I'd love to hear your definition of it. I think contract workers are contingent workers, is that right?"

"Yes, they are, and you'd be surprised to learn how many types exist today. No doubt we'll be adding more to the list in the next few years. Some of the most common types of contingent workers are independent consultants or contract workers, who are typically hired for specific projects. An emerging trend is the virtual assistant. As small businesses grow, they typically reach a point where they need some type of administrative support. We've all likely experienced virtual agents, popping up to offer support when we're online, and while bots are commonly used for that purpose, there will always be some need for humans. We're seeing more and more websites like Fiverr popping up, where you can easily access freelancers, retired professionals, or even 'moonlighting' employees who have a side hustle. And then of course, there is the fractional worker—a C-suite level executive who provides their services to multiple organizations, often small businesses who either don't need a full-time chief financial officer or chief information officer or can't afford one. Closely related to that is the interim worker—the professional who provides their services on a temporary basis—often to fill a maternity leave, leave of absence, or a vacancy."

Alex was shaking his head. "I had no idea how many variations there are!"

Mark chuckled. "Oops. I likely got carried away again with all the examples. But yes, I hear that a lot. And that doesn't include all the contract trade workers out there."

Alex sat back in his chair. "This has been helpful. You've given me a lot of options to consider as a startup. You certainly are knowledgeable!"

Mark nodded. "What can I say—I love my job, studying workforce trends. It's interesting to observe how the global workplace has shifted since the pandemic. There's a whole team of researchers at our company who focus specifically on the employee experience and how expectations are changing. We're seeing an increasing percentage of employees looking for more meaning in their work or opportunities to align with their purpose; more flexibility in terms of when they work and where they work; and more challenges and experiences to grow. All that translates into a potential explosion in the number of new business registrations we may see in the next decade."

"It's great to meet someone so passionate about workforce trends. I'm curious though—what do you think about the portfolio career trend?"

Mark smiled. "Ah yes—the original question. I believe Charles Handy was a smart man, and the portfolio trend will continue. The beauty of the gig economy is that there are multiple ways for people to make money, and it's getting easier and easier for contingent workers to get connected with employers who need their services."

"That's exciting news. At the same time, that makes it more difficult to decide what kind of business to start, with so many options."

"You don't have to worry about that just yet," Janine suggested. "Once you have a clearer vision of your purpose and who your ideal client will be, the decision of how best to reach that potential client will be a lot easier."

Alex turned to Janine. "You started telling me earlier that you have a portfolio career. Does one of your businesses involve being a contingent worker?"

Janine smiled. "As a matter of fact, yes. When I decided it was time to leave the firm, I approached my boss about continuing my relationship with the firm on a contract basis. I'm so lucky that my previous employer was supportive, and so one of my jobs or businesses involves being an independent consultant doing the same work that I've done for decades. That role takes up about half of my time. My second job is providing support to startups to help them choose their business idea, to develop a plan, and to get going, which I absolutely love doing."

Alex shook his head. "I'm curious. If you love the startup coaching role, why aren't you focusing all your time on that business?"

Janine pressed her hand to her chest. "The startup coaching gig is my purpose—no question. But the consulting gig is my paycheck—at least, in the early days until I can get the business established."

Mark chuckled. "That's an interesting way of describing it."

Janine threw up her hands. "It doesn't mean that I'm not completely committed to building my business. When I'm spending half my time on it, I'm committed 100 percent to what I'm doing. It just means that I like having the cash flow to fund that business venture, along with some personal travel. That way I'm not dipping into my retirement savings. And with that money coming in, I'm more confident making investments in the business that I think will help me in the long run, like spending money on the marketing activities I think my business needs."

Alex's face lit up. "I love it! Now I understand your comment earlier when you said that juggling two businesses is actually helping your financial situation."

Janine nodded. "Exactly. When I hear my clients say that they would love to start a business but they're not sure if they can swing it financially with young kids at home, I always suggest that they consider a portfolio career. When I do, I see the relief in their faces. They realize they might not have to wait until the kids are grown, or until the house is paid off, or until they're close to retirement. A contingent role can provide them with the cash flow they need to pay the bills while they build a business. It's liberating for many of them."

"I can totally relate to that! All the discussions that Rachel and I have had about my starting a business have been about the question of WHEN can we afford to do this? It didn't even occur to me to have a side gig—a paycheck, as you say, that minimizes the financial impact of the decision."

Janine smiled. "I'm glad that a portfolio career is something you'll be exploring when you do your business planning. I have some clients who take on a part-time job, others who do contract work. Some of them have their services listed on sites like Fiverr. As Mark said, it's exciting how many options exist today."

Mark had been listening intently. "Congratulations again, Janine, on your decision to start your business. I can hear in your voice that it's working well for you, and I'm not surprised to hear that you've been advising your startup clients to consider a portfolio career. As I'm sure you already know, the main downside of that strategy is that realistically, it will take you longer to build your business because you're juggling two businesses, as opposed to one."

Janine nodded. "I can't disagree with that. That's why I always have a conversation with my clients about the trade-off. If it takes you two years longer or five years longer to build that business, is it worth it to start that business today—as opposed to waiting 10 years, until the kids are off to university?"

Mark looked at Alex. "She's right!" He turned to Janine. "Good for you for deciding you weren't willing to wait any longer to realize your entrepreneurial dream. The reality is that your previous employer was likely desperate to have you stay in any capacity, so it's a win for them—they don't have to scramble to find someone to replace you. And it's a win for you—you enjoy more flexibility and likely a more lucrative arrangement. And it's a win for your previous workers' clients who continue to get access to you. Sounds like a win, win, win to me!"

"Absolutely!" Janine replied with a huge grin. "Everyone wins!"

Alex looked at Janine. "I totally understand why a portfolio career makes sense—the purpose and the paycheck!" He then looked over at Mark again. "I'm so glad we bumped into you today. You've taught me that there are so many more ways to make money in this gig economy than I even realized. You've given me lots to think about. This dream of business ownership and working in flip flops and shorts every day might be a realistic expectation after all."

"That reminds me, Alex—I have a colleague who is doing some interesting research on the startup CEO role. Lucy may have some additional insights that could help you define your path. If you'd like, I'd be happy to introduce you to her."

Alex's eyes widened with excitement. "That would be awesome! I'm interested in gathering all the information I can get my hands on at this stage. Now that I know that I don't need to choose one purpose and one path, I want to explore all the possible options."

Lesson 7 Summary

Key Takeaways:

There are so many ways to make money in today's economy. As a result, there is a wide range of business owner roles to consider for your startup business, including the following:

- Contract workers or independent consultants
- Virtual assistants who provide small businesses with part-time support
- Virtual assistants who provide on-line chat support when bots are not sufficient
- Freelancers
- Contract trade workers
- Retired professionals
- Moonlighting employees
- Fractional leaders who provide small business with part-time executive level support
- Interim workers who provide temporary support such as for a leave of absence or a vacancy

You might decide that a portfolio career that involves taking on more than one role is the ideal fit for you.

Question to Consider:

Which of these business owner roles are you interested in exploring?

Part C:

Discovering Your Polar Star

Lesson 8

Don't Believe the Fairy Tale About Overnight Success

Two minutes before nine o'clock, Alex joined the Zoom call that Mark arranged for him to meet Lucy, Mark's colleague. As they were introducing themselves, Alex noticed that Lucy had a certificate hanging on the wall behind her. He squinted and noticed it was a doctoral degree.

"Wow—Mark didn't mention that you're a doctor."

Lucy looked behind her. "Oh—I always forget that's there. Well, I'm not a medical doctor. My doctoral thesis was on the topic of culture, which is why I'm passionate about studying the workforce and workplace."

"I've never heard of a PhD in culture. That's so cool! Mark tells me that you're researching startup owners."

"That's one of my areas of specialization. Mark mentioned that you're considering starting your own business and might benefit from hearing about some of the research and trends we're finding."

"That was nice of him to give you some background on my situation."

Lucy smiled. "Congratulations on your decision to start a business. That's exciting."

"Thank you. Yes, the word exciting definitely comes to mind. Truthfully, scary also comes to mind. You see, I've never started a business before, so I'm not sure what to expect."

Lucy sat back in her chair. "That makes you normal." They both laughed.

Lucy continued, "Honestly, there are some pervasive myths out there about startups. I don't know how anyone can have a realistic expectation of what life will be like. Let me share with you the most damaging misperceptions that I see."

"That would be awesome!"

"Well, I don't want to burst your bubble, but myth #1 relates to a flexible schedule. Some people hear on social media that there are entrepreneurs who are running successful businesses working less than five or ten hours a week. What they don't typically tell you is that they worked very long hours for countless years before they eventually landed on that flexible schedule. They might not tell you their secret of having automated sales, marketing, and distribution systems for their products or services. In other words, no startup owner ever achieved that level of automation without first working extremely hard, and likely didn't have a ten-hour work week in their first year."

Alex thought about his desire to drive Joey to and from school every day. "How many hours does the typical startup owner work?"

"Great question! Depending on the research study, you'll read that between 50 or 60 hours a week is common, and the smaller the organization, the longer the week, particularly for solo entrepreneurs who choose to wear most hats."[30]

"I see. So, while I might be setting my own hours, the reality is that if I want to be able to drop Joey off at basketball after school, I'll be working in the evenings, not to mention on weekends."

Lucy shrugged her shoulders. "You'll need to decide for yourself what your vision for your ideal schedule looks like—the hours you want to work and the days you want to work. I sometimes hear people have a goal to work a four-day work week. No Fridays, for example. The average entrepreneur may work 50 hours, but you might say that you're only prepared to put in 25 hours a week, in which case you would need to temper your expectation about how long it will take you to build that business, right? If you're okay with taking twice as long to achieve your goal, then there's nothing wrong with that schedule."

"True. I got myth #1. If I'm not willing to invest as much time, I shouldn't expect the same reward. Or at least, don't expect the reward to come as quickly. How long DOES it take to build a successful business, assuming for a moment that I was prepared to work 50 or 60 hours a week?"

Lucy gave Alex a virtual high five. "Ah—great question. Myth #2 relates to how long it really takes to build a successful business."

"Are you about to tell me that my dreams of being an overnight success aren't likely to be real?" They both laughed.

"You're obviously ready for me to bust myth #2. Depending upon which research study you pick up, you'll hear that it typically takes seven to ten years, or even longer, to achieve success.[31] Of course, that depends on how you define success, what type of business you're starting, whether you have any experience in that area, and so many other factors."

"That's much longer than I would have guessed."

Lucy nodded. "That's because we typically don't see all the hard work that went on behind the scenes before a startup owner emerges in the spotlight, seemingly overnight. Jeff Bezos once said, 'All *overnight* success takes 10 years.' Just look at Elon Musk—it was 10 years before he had his first profitable quarter with Tesla.[32] I could go on and on with examples."

"I'm not surprised—everyone talks about how much work it takes to start up a business. It's just that you hear stories about some people going viral on social media who are seemingly famous in less than a year."

Lucy shook her head. "Alex, I'm willing to admit that there are exceptions to every truth, so there may in fact be a very small handful of people who have experienced a good level of success in a reasonably short time, perhaps due to good timing, or luck, or both. More often than not, if you spoke to those people, you would learn about their failed attempts with a different business, or even with a different product offering before they evolved it, and then it finally took off. But those instances are extremely rare, and never happen without first putting in a tremendous amount of work."

"So you're telling me not to count on being a billionaire by the time I'm 40 years old."

Lucy chuckled. "Too funny. Actually, that's myth #3. You'd be surprised how many people believe that if you haven't become a billionaire by the time you're 40, then it won't happen. Part of the reason why is because they think of technology entrepreneurs like Bill Gates, Steve Jobs, and Mark Zuckerberg, who all started billion-dollar companies while they were in their 20's."

"I must admit that the billionaires I think of are all in the technology sector. Perhaps because that's the sector I work in."

"As I say, you're not alone, Alex. These public personalities are top of mind, so it's understandable that people have a misperception about the typical age of a billionaire. After all, the kind of hard work you need to put in requires a lot of energy that we arguably have more of when we're young."

"True—that's easy to rationalize."

Lucy leaned forward. "Most people would be surprised to learn that less than 10 percent of all billionaires are under 50. The actual average age of all global billionaires is 67."[33]

"Really?"

"Yes. According to the research, almost half of the roughly 3,000 global billionaires are between the ages of 50 and 70, and more than 40 percent are over 70 years old."[34]

"Wow! I never would have guessed that. On the other hand, achieving that level of success obviously takes time and experience."

Lucy smiled. "Yes, becoming a billionaire typically takes time, but don't let that discourage you, Alex. Every one of them started out just like you, with a dream to build a business. Don't forget that!"

Alex smiled. "Thanks for that. This has been a really helpful conversation to manage my expectations. I see now that I need to be prepared to play the long game."

"I like that. The long game means that it's not unusual to take a couple of years to refine your product or service to meet your clients' needs. And then it could realistically take another couple of years to design sales and marketing systems for reaching and landing new clients. Many startup owners will tell you that it took several years before they felt like they finally figured things out and could start to scale the business."

Alex slumped down in his chair. "Thanks for breaking down the first few years of the seven-to-ten-year journey. I suppose we really don't appreciate the entrepreneurial path until we've lived it. If I'm being honest, it sounds like a long haul."

"Yes, it can be. That's one of the reasons why some startups choose to have a partner. They're looking for someone to share the risk with, along with the financial reward. It may be a friend, colleague, or family member that they trust, and often they look for someone with complementary skills."

"So, are you suggesting that's a good way to go?"

"No—please don't take that as advice. There are pros and cons to partnerships, and the truth is that 70% of all partnerships fail."[35]

"Oh—I see. Why does that happen?"

Lucy shrugged. "There are lots of reasons, but some of the most common I've read about are related to communication issues or disagreements about what a fair distribution of the wealth looks like."[36]

Alex nodded. "I would have assumed that profits would be split fifty-fifty in a partnership. No? I suppose if both partners aren't contributing equally, I can see how that might lead to a difference of opinion."

"Yes, an equal split is common, but there are other arrangements that can be negotiated. You're exactly right—one party may not be living up to the agreement, from the perspective of the other partner. Also, it's not uncommon for people's life circumstances to change, and they no longer want to, or are able to, maintain that level of commitment to the business."[37]

Alex thought about his own personal situation. "Rachel and I have talked about having a child together. I can see how our life circumstances will likely change in the next few years if that happens, which means I may not have the same time available to build up a business down the road."

"That's a great example of a life-changing event that could impact the time you're able to spend on the business."

Alex placed both hands on his head, as if to stop it from exploding. "Boy—I realize now that I need to develop a life plan, and not just a business plan. And Rachel needs to be involved in that planning in a significant way."

"It seems you have a realistic expectation of the magnitude of the task of starting a business. I certainly hope that understanding what it takes to build a successful business hasn't dampened your enthusiasm in any way."

Alex sat up. "Oh, no, not one bit. Believe it or not, I actually feel more confident. Because of this conversation, I think I'll be more prepared for the journey."

Lesson 8 Summary

Key Takeaways:
There are several myths that contribute to unrealistic expectations about the startup owner profile and lifestyle:

- The myth that a 10 to 20-hour work week is feasible. Most startup owners work 50, 60 or even more hours a week for the first few years before they finally establish repeatable processes and can automate their operations.
- The myth about overnight success. Most startups achieve success after seven to ten years or longer.
- The myth that the typical billionaire is a technology company owner in his mid-30's. The average age of billionaires is 67.
- The myth that partnerships will enable a business to be successful twice as fast. The truth is that 70% of business partnerships fail, typically due to communication issues or misaligned expectations.

Questions to Consider:
What is your ideal work schedule? What days of the week do you want to work? What hours do you want to work?

Lesson 9

Don't Fall Into the Common Traps that Contribute to Most Small Business Failures

L ucy slouched down in her chair. "I'm glad you're feeling more prepared to start a business. That will certainly give you a leg up on your competition."

"Why do you believe I would have a competitive advantage, Lucy?"

"As I mentioned, the small business failure rate is quite high. What do you know about the reasons for most small business failures?"

"Well, I've heard something about finances; perhaps the lack of funding?"

"Yes. Depending on the research report you're looking at, some will suggest that poor cash flow management or a lack of startup funding are key contributors to failure. You might have also heard a reference to a lack of market knowledge and failure to develop a business plan as some of the reasons that come up repeatedly in the research."[38]

Alex straightened up. "Yes, those both make sense."

"I'd be happy to share my perspective, and I think it will surprise you! I'm going to share some completely different reasons, and what I believe is the number one secret to success. Ready?"

"Wow! That sounds amazing. You bet I'm ready!"

Lucy smiled. "Speaking of ready, that's actually the number one reason for business failure. The individual was not prepared to take on that top job."

Alex had a perplexed look on his face. "Really?"

"It's true. The reality is that most of the CEOs who were interviewed by McKinsey partners in the book *CEO Excellence* admitted that they weren't clear about the work they would be doing in that top job.[39] When we're not clear about what work we'll be doing, how do we know if we have the skills to effectively complete the required tasks?"

"Wow—I'm surprised that leaders in that top job said that they didn't know what work they would be doing. Did that surprise you too?"

Lucy paused to reflect on the question. "The CEOs were being honest. In hindsight, they were able to see that they had not been sufficiently prepared."

"Do you think that's true of startup CEOs or just corporate CEOs?"

Lucy nodded. "Good question Alex. Let me ask you— what percentage of startup owners do you think have a business plan?"

Alex tried to recall what he had heard about that. "I think it's a low percentage, am I right?"

"Yes. Depending on the research study, you might have seen 20 percent—perhaps it was a bit lower or higher."[40] Most don't do the business planning work to get prepared."

Alex shook his head. "It's no wonder the failure rate for small businesses is so high."

Lucy nodded. "To be fair, I believe many startup owners do SOME level of planning. A marketing plan is likely the most common, but I typically see plans that include very surface-level details about the customer's need and the proposed solution or product offering to meet the need. I don't often see any market research that attempts to estimate the size of the market, for example. And there are many aspects to running a business that are often not even considered by the owner before they get started."

Alex shrugged. "So I'm not the only one who doesn't like the idea of doing sales planning?"

Lucy smiled. "Yes—you're not alone. But a self-assessment of one's skills is critical to preparation for the role."

"I can see why that would be important! Are you suggesting that business planning should include an assessment of a startup owner's skills?"

"Exactly right! I'm glad that you made that connection. It's impossible to assess whether you have the skills to do the work if you haven't spent any time thinking about the work. How you will sell, for example. Face-to-face selling requires a certain set of skills and online selling requires a completely different set of skills. When startup owners avoid the topic of selling and don't decide about the type of selling they'll be doing, they miss the opportunity to do a self-assessment to reveal their blind spots, which can create challenges once they start the business."

"I get it. I'm going to find out about my blind spot sooner or later. It sounds like you're suggesting that sooner is a good choice. And yet that's not the norm, is it?"

Chuckling, Lucy responded, "No, it's just not our nature. Be honest, how much do you enjoy performance reviews?"

Alex laughed, "Okay. Who wants to hear what they're not good at?"

Lucy smiled. "Exactly! Obviously, there are exceptions to that rule. Many high performers would say that they welcome constructive feedback because when they know what their weaknesses or blind spots are, they can work on those areas. I hope you're seeing that successful startup owners do what they can to anticipate their future and how they need to learn and grow."

"100 percent!"

Lucy sat back. "Great! Another reason for the high failure rate is the complexity of the job."[41]

"Interesting! What do you mean by complexity?"

"We know that the scope of the top job is far broader than any other job that exists in an organization. Do you agree with that?"

"I think so. Basically that every department leader has their own scope of responsibility, but the CEO has to be concerned about everyone's scope."

"That's exactly right. One of the key findings that you'll read about if you pick up that book authored by the McKinsey partners is that many CEOs struggled, particularly in their first year, because of the scope of the work—as the top job, you're accountable for everything.[42] When you think about it, the CEO must wear every hat in the company; the accountant, the salesperson, the product developer...you get the idea."

"That makes sense. At the beginning, an entrepreneur must do it all. Right?"

"That's right. When the McKinsey partners embarked on their CEO research, they didn't find a CEO who was great at EVERYTHING. Instead, they discovered that successful CEOs are excellent in a few areas and are solid in the others."[43]

Alex smiled. "Interesting. At the firm where I work, we say that our best partners are generalists. They may have a deep expertise in one area like technology—I think Janine referred to it as being a 'mile deep,' but the best partners are at least an 'inch deep' in almost every area of the business model. That's why they're the best advisors."

"That's a great analogy. If by being an 'inch deep' you mean that they have a solid footing or foundation, that certainly applies to the best CEOs. I like it! And just because you have knowledge in a particular area, it doesn't mean that you should try to do everything."

Alex sat up. "Oh—that's a good point."

"That was one of the key findings of the McKinsey research, which is related to another reason why many small businesses fail. When interviewed, CEOs admitted that the vast amount of work was one of the key challenges related to the top job.[44] Failure to delegate can be a costly mistake."

Alex shrugged. "But at the beginning, I won't have anyone to delegate to."

Lucy smiled. "Well, yes and no. As a solo entrepreneur, you may not have any employees to delegate to on day one. However, I could argue that there are external resources you can delegate or direct work toward. We often see that startup owners aren't always willing or comfortable doing that as early as they could be."

"I think I might struggle with that. Hiring is a big decision, and cost."

"Exactly! Some entrepreneurs grow their business to a certain level and then reach a plateau, many because they struggle with delegation or letting go of control. For example, they may be reluctant to hire a virtual assistant soon enough. As a result, they often spend more time on administrative tasks that someone else could be doing, and not enough time on selling or other client-facing activities that are needed to grow the business."

Alex's eyes widened. "To be honest, I can see the temptation to procrastinate when it comes to selling, so convincing myself that reformatting training materials is more important at that moment in time."

Lucy laughed. "Yes, it's easy to find excuses for doing work we don't like, isn't it? We also know that when startup owners aren't working on the right things, success can be delayed, limited, or worse. Getting into the habit of regularly asking yourself, 'Is this the best use of my time?' can be helpful for identifying opportunities for you to free yourself up to do more value-add tasks like selling."

"I hear ya."

Lucy chuckled. "There is sometimes another solution, and that's to automate certain activities. For example, startup owners have lots of tool options today that automate things like collecting names and addresses to build an email list, sending out freebies in exchange for that contact information, accepting payments, or even sending new customers some course materials. In other words, there is so much manual work that can be avoided with some very cost-effective systems and tools."

"Thanks for those strategies for staying focused on the right things. Those were really practical examples of automations and tasks I might need to delegate."

Lucy nodded. "It sounds like you have a good handle on that second reason for failure—the scope of the role. According to the McKinsey partners who authored *CEO Excellence*, another reason why many CEOs struggle is due to the isolation or the solitary nature of the role."[45]

Alex thought about his own situation. "I don't think that'll be an issue for me. After all, I have the support of my family."

Lucy shook her head. "Social contact isn't the same as contact with a colleague. When CEOs find themselves in that top job for the first time, they no longer have a peer group to consult with when challenges occur."

"I hadn't really thought about it from that perspective. I suppose that having no one to answer to ALSO means that there is no one to turn to for answers."

"Well said! Another reason why a startup owner may experience isolation is that it typically takes more time to build up the business than we think. In the words of Tony Robbins, we tend to overestimate what we think we can do in a year and underestimate what we can do in ten.[46] Many startup owners aren't mentally prepared for the long period of isolation before they start getting clients or hiring employees."

Alex had pictured himself working at home as a startup owner but had focused more on the flip flops and shorts he would be wearing. He really hadn't thought about what he would be doing all day. "It's funny. As much as we complain about all the Zoom calls, the only thing that seems worse than back-to-back meetings is a week with absolutely no meetings. No clients to talk to. No colleagues to chat with."

Lucy leaned forward in her chair. "I can see that the reality of the work environment of a startup owner is beginning to sink in. Again, social media tends to glamorize the lifestyle of the entrepreneur. The good news is that you're already ahead of most startup owners, Alex."

"Why do you say that?"

"Here you are, learning about the journey. The lightbulb went on for you BEFORE you started up the business. Most startup owners don't do this amount of work before to get started, and as a result, aren't prepared for the emotional aspects of the journey."

"I guess not. After all, you mentioned that the small business failure rate is still high."

Lucy smiled. "The other good news is that you CAN do something about it. My advice to you is to plan some social interaction into your week. The point is that when you have self-awareness about the level of social contact that you enjoy, you can proactively do something to avoid those feelings of isolation."

Alex sat up. "Good point. I know other independent consultants and contractors. I hadn't thought about the benefits of networking with them, from a social perspective. They'll also be great coaches for me."

Lucy gave Alex another virtual high five. "That's an awesome idea. There are so many benefits of having a strong support network. That can help mitigate against imposter syndrome too, which is particularly common in the first year of starting up a business. You know, that fear that others will see us as a fraud. It stems from feelings of self-doubt. When you're first starting up, it's common to have moments when we don't feel qualified to be running a business. I've noticed that imposter syndrome is common among people who have worked in a large corporate environment, before starting up their own business. It's particularly prevalent among individuals whose identities were tied up in their corporate roles. We also see it's common among high achievers, who have high standards for themselves."

Alex drifted back to his childhood, and memories of talking with his father at the dinner table. He recalled hearing his father use phrases like, 'My tiny business' when talking about his store. Alex remembered how his father minimized his own accomplishments, and he never really understood why until now.

"I think I know what you're referring to. Now that you've put a name to it—imposter syndrome—that was probably how my father felt when he would describe his problems as 'small-time' or his business as 'the junior league.' It always bothered me that he never saw his business as successful and yet his customers seemed to describe him as a hero."

Lucy's smile was full of empathy. "I'm sorry to hear that your father struggled with imposter syndrome. I can hear that he was a hero in your eyes. He was also very normal. That's the message that I want you to take away from this story. You see, it's common for people running their own business to feel like they're 'playing small,' despite how talented or competent they are, or how others might perceive them."

Alex shook his head. "Boy—I sure see how this imposter syndrome impacted my father's confidence. What can I do to avoid following in my father's footsteps?"

"You might be surprised at this first piece of advice. Recognize that your business IS small."

"What?"

Lucy smiled. "It's easy to overlook that EVERY business was small when it first got started. Second, it will be helpful to have supporters remind you about the many reasons why you will succeed—your courage, your knowledge, your commitment. Third, when you take action during those times when you're feeling small, it will help build up the confidence you need to overcome imposter syndrome. In other words, keep going!"

"Thanks, Lucy—I'll be sure to ask my family to look for those signs of imposter syndrome. And I'll ask them to remind me about having realistic expectations about the size of my business on day one. Hopefully I'll be lucky enough to grow the business."

Lucy smiled. "You're a quick study, Alex. Yes, I hope you feel comfortable asking loved ones for help. However, on the topic of luck?"

"Are you going to tell me that the most successful startups aren't lucky—it's all skill?"

Lucy leaned forward and laughed. "There's no proof that shows that the successful startups are luckier or smarter—in fact, they fail more often than most unsuccessful startups."

"That doesn't make any sense to me."

Lucy smiled. "Many people wrongly assume that successful startup owners fail less often. The opposite is more accurate—they tend to fail more often because they're willing to try new things more often. Look at Thomas Edison. Do you know how many failed attempts he had before inventing the light bulb?"

"Hmm. You're probably going to tell me he failed 100 times."

Lucy shook her head. "Not quite. It was actually one thousand times!"[47]

Alex's eyes widened. "Wow! Imagine if he had walked around for six months after every failure feeling sorry for himself, instead of trying the next idea. We'd be in the dark, literally!"

"That's funny! And true! That's a great lesson to take away from that story. Successful entrepreneurs tend to fail fast, learn, and then move on quickly to the next attempt. They tend to be more resilient than unsuccessful startups."

Alex lowered his head. "I'm not sure that I've always demonstrated resilience in the past. I tend to get pretty discouraged easily. So why do you believe in me?"

Lucy smiled. "Don't be too hard on yourself—it's a common reaction to want to quit after experiencing a failure. But the good news is that resilience is something you can build."

"I'm surprised! I thought we're either born with it or not."

Lucy chuckled. "No—there's no evidence of that. It's a skill that you can learn. You see, successful startup owners recognize that they are on a learning journey. When that's your mindset, you will see failure as part of the process."

"Wow. You're making failure sound like a good thing."

"Well, if you believe, like Edison did, that the more you fail, the closer you are to success, then yes! I would say it's a good thing. It means you're trying," Lucy added with a wink.

Alex smiled. "We used to say that about skiing. If you're not falling, you're not trying hard enough."

Lucy smiled. "The same is true of running a business. Remember I told you that I would be sharing with you some less published reasons for small business failure, and I promised I would share with you the secret to a successful startup, from my perspective?"

Alex sat up. "That's right. What's the secret?"

Lucy paused and then said, "It's DON'T QUIT! Keep trying new things, and evolving your product or service offering UNTIL you get it right. I believe the number one reason why most startups fail is they stop trying. At some point, they give up. So, the secret is, simply don't stop."

Alex chuckled. "I like that secret. I'm writing it down, so I remember that every day."

"That's a great idea. It's easy for high performers to have unrealistic expectations that they'll get most things right from day one. They're often conditioned to believe that failure is a bad thing or something to be avoided. Instead, condition yourself to think of failure as an important step in the learning process. That way, you'll be less likely to react negatively and to be hard on yourself when you make a mistake. Consequently, you'll be less likely to succumb to that temptation to quit."

Alex sat back, feeling relieved. "So, the secret to success is having the right mindset. I just have to tell myself I'm not failing, I'm just learning. I'm not failing, I'm just learning."

Lucy chuckled. "That's the idea! Mindset is a great start, but you also need to follow that up with good preparation, right?"

Alex nodded. "100 percent! I have to be honest—I wasn't expecting to have a conversation about mindset from a PhD."

Lucy winked. "A PhD in culture, don't forget. The biggest battle that you'll face will be with yourself and your own mindset. As I mentioned, I see so often that startup owners aren't prepared because they have unrealistic expectations about the journey, and then when those expectations aren't met, they get discouraged and quit."

Alex nodded. "This meeting has far exceeded my expectations. I can't thank you enough for spending this time with me. I can't wait to tell Janine about our discussion."

Lesson 9 Summary

Key Takeaways:
There are several reasons for the high small business failure rate. The traditional responses you read about are a lack of funding, poor cash flow management, lack of business planning, and lack of market knowledge. However, the reasons you may not know about are:
- They aren't clear about the work they will be doing
- They don't have a solid foundation on all aspects of the business
- They lack self-awareness about their skill or knowledge gaps
- They aren't prepared for the complexity of the role
- They aren't prepared for the vast amount of work
- They aren't prepared for the isolation of the role or lack of peers
- They quit

To increase your chance at success:
- **Contemplate** all aspects of your business and the work that you will be doing
- **Evaluate** your strengths and the gaps in your ability to perform the work. Build your self-awareness and address your gaps

- **Delegate** the 'lower-value' work that someone else can do. Just because you're good at something doesn't mean it's the best use of your time
- **Automate** activities where it is cost-effective to do so. Minimize the amount of manual effort to improve efficiency

The most successful startup owners aren't great at everything. They are excellent at a few areas and have a solid foundation in all the rest.

Question to Consider:
What areas of business are you the least familiar with?

Lesson 10

Don't Be Afraid to Have a Goal or to Define Success

When Alex got off the call, he sent a quick email to Mark thanking him for the introduction. Then, he sent a text to Janine. It read, *A life-changing conversation.*

A few seconds after he pushed send on the text and put his phone down, he heard it ring. He could see it was Janine calling.

Alex chuckled. "Hey there—I thought that might be you."

"Well, your text certainly got my attention. I just had to call to find out what was so life-changing about your conversation."

Alex flopped down on the couch. "Where to start? I had some really unrealistic expectations about the lifestyle of a typical startup owner—how much they work and how long it takes to establish a business. I also would have said that the average age of billionaires was closer to 37 rather than the actual age of 67."

"Is that true? I wouldn't have guessed that either."

"I know, right? Social media is filled with pictures of 30-something-year-olds who own jets, Lamborghinis, and huge estate homes on the ocean. Exposure to those sites can really raise unrealistic expectations about the kind of lifestyle most entrepreneurs have."

"Very true! When I'm coaching startup owners, some people believe that overnight success is real!"

Alex shook his head, feeling a bit deflated. "It certainly was a humbling discussion."

"Don't feel bad, Alex. As you say, social media paints an unrealistic picture of the kind of success that startups can expect. Besides, the opposite situation is worse."

Alex tried to imagine what the opposite might be. "Hmm, you got me—what's the opposite?"

"Having no goal or expectation at all."

"Ah—I get it, but why is that actually worse than having unrealistic expectations?"

"In the words of Denzel Washington—'dreams without goals are just dreams.'[48]

Alex grinned. "I've never heard that. That's inspirational!"

"Denzel seems to be suggesting that if we have a dream to start a business and don't take the smallest action of attaching a goal to it, it'll never happen."

"So let me get this straight. There's value in setting a goal—and it doesn't matter what that goal is?"

Janine paused to consider the question. "Have you ever heard that quote from Zig Ziglar, 'If you aim at nothing, you will hit it every time?'"[49]

"Sure, but you don't think it's just an expression?"

"I think the point he was making as a high-performance coach is that if you aim low, don't be surprised at how little you achieve. Conversely, by setting a stretch goal for yourself, you're demonstrating a higher level of ambition, and therefore more likely to achieve a higher level of success."

"That makes sense. Obviously, I'll aim high, but how important is it that I have a specific goal in mind? Is it enough that I have a rough idea in my head?"

"Let me answer that question this way. In your opinion, if you were flying to New York, is it good enough if the pilot had a rough idea of where they would land?"

Alex smiled. "That's an interesting analogy."

"It's true. When startup owners don't have a specific target in mind, they tend to drift along aimlessly, just like that plane that is off course most of the time. Without the clarity of a desired destination or goal, I've seen many entrepreneurs get frustrated by the lack of progress they're making, and inevitably quit."

Alex thought back to their conversation at the coffee shop last week. "I do remember you mentioning how easy it is to say yes to clients, which can take you down a rabbit hole of doing work that isn't aligned with your purpose, so I can see how a business might drift if the goal isn't clear."

"Sadly, that can easily happen. Another implication of not having a specific target is that you won't have a measure of success, which means you're not assessing your progress and you're robbing yourself of the satisfaction that comes with achieving an aggressive goal that you set for yourself."

Alex nodded. "I can see how that sense of accomplishment only comes with having a tangible target."

"That's right, and you're also robbing yourself of the opportunity to celebrate those little wins along the way. My celebration treat is ice cream—I'm sure you'll have your own." They both laughed.

"I realize that not everyone places the same importance on tracking progress," Janine said. "I do now, though—I learned that lesson the hard way."

"What do you mean?"

"I told you about that business I started over 20 years ago, the one where I wasn't clear about my purpose or my why. Well, I also didn't really set a goal—at least, not a business goal. My husband and I came up with the name Lakehall for the company because we had a personal goal to buy a lake house at the time. And when I reached the point of having enough money to pay cash for a lake house, I just folded the business."

Alex's eyes widened. "Wow that sounds like a successful business to me."

"Looking back, I could have easily made ten times more than that in the business, but I gave up after that personal goal was achieved. I never defined success for the business, so I never really pushed myself to strive for that next level which I know NOW I could have achieved."

Alex could hear the regret in Janine's voice. "I can see the implications of not having a specific goal. Why do you suppose we're so hesitant to commit to a goal?"

"I think you hit the nail on the head with the word hesitant. For many people, it's a commitment, and we're uncomfortable declaring a target that we'll be held accountable for—unsure if we can achieve it."

"I suppose we could always set a goal and not share it."

"We're still accountable to ourselves. And there's a lot of research that shows that when we achieve the goals that we set for ourselves, that builds our confidence. That alone is a tremendous benefit of setting a goal."

"I can see that. Well maybe there could be a goal that I'll push myself to achieve, and another goal that I share with others?"

"That's certainly one approach."

Alex smiled sheepishly. "I might not even share the real target with Rachel! Just kidding—she knows instantly when I'm lying and would be able to drag the real goal out of me."

Janine chuckled. "Too funny. It sounds like you and Rachel are a good team. There are many benefits of having an accountability partner—someone who will keep you focused on your goal."

"I like that term—Rachel is my accountability partner."

"Alex, I'm curious—do you imagine sharing your goal with anyone besides Rachel?"

"Hmmm. I hadn't really thought about it. Is there merit in doing that too?"

"You'll hear a lot of varying perspectives about whether it's a good idea to share your goals. On the one hand, some people advocate that we shouldn't tell anyone—our results will communicate our goals. Others believe that our level of commitment to achieving a goal increases when we share it with others. What do you believe?"

"Are we talking about sharing the goal with a handful of family and friends, or are we talking about broadcasting my goal on social media?"

Alex could practically hear Janine cringe over the line. "Certainly not on social media."

Alex paused to consider the idea. "Can you imagine if I had announced to the world on Instagram that I would be driving a Ferrari or sailing my yacht in one year? I would have been ridiculed publicly. Most of my friends and colleagues are on Instagram—they never would have let me live that down."

Janine laughed. "So true. Good thing Lucy set you straight about how unrealistic overnight success would be, before that happened."

Alex nodded. "Exactly! Honestly, I'm not sure. What do you think of the idea of sharing goals with family and friends?"

Janine took a deep breath. "Well, I learned a tough lesson about having unrealistic expectations about how supportive friends would be. When I was in Grade 5, our teacher went around the room, asking each of us to share our dream with the rest of the class. When it was my turn, I shared that my dream was to win a gold medal in the Olympics. Every kid in that classroom burst out laughing at me. Although the teacher scolded them, the damage was done. That traumatic moment taught me that some people will try to kill your dreams."

Alex was horrified. "You've never shared that story. I'm so sorry, Janine—that must have been horrible."

"To be honest, Alex—I firmly believe it's the reason why I'm so passionate about helping people to realize their dreams."

Alex lowered his head. "Now that we're talking about it, there are certain family members who already think I'm foolish for wanting to start a business. Last week, my sister said she thinks I'm too young."

"I'm sorry to hear that you don't have the support of some of your family members. My advice to you is to be selective about who you share your goal with, and who you talk with about your business. You'll discover, like I did, that some friends and family will be jealous of your ambition, and the more successful you are, the worse that behavior might be. Be prepared for haters on social media and skeptics among your family and friends. But promise me, Alex—you won't let anyone kill your dream."

Alex smiled. "Thank you for that warning. I think goal setting is something I'll do for myself, anyway."

"I believe that too. It gives you something to aim at—to help you visualize success."

"Does that mean you believe in the power of visualization?"

"If you've done any reading about the power of visualization, you'll know that professional athletes use it all the time to help them achieve a state of peak performance.[50] For an athlete, visualization involves rehearsing a successful outcome over and over, whether that's a touchdown in football or shooting that three-pointer in basketball."

Alex looked skeptical. "Hmm. I'm not sure if I'm a proponent of visualization. My dad used to say that it doesn't take the place of hard work."

"Your father was a smart man, and I would be willing to bet that professional athletes who use visualization would agree that picturing success alone doesn't win football or basketball games. They might argue that visualization helps to identify a pattern of success behaviors, but you need to practice those behaviors consistently and diligently to be successful. Does that resonate?"

"100 percent!"

"You know, when I first set my goal, I wrote down that definition of success on a white board in my bedroom that I looked at every day. I wrote in red marker the words 'helping thousands of startup owners.' It helped me stay focused on that dream while I was still in my corporate job, struggling to get out of bed."

"That's a great idea! Although I think I'll post mine on the fridge. Now that I'm working from home, I'm WAYYY more likely to visit that during the day than my bedroom."

Janine laughed. "Whatever works for you! You've got the idea that a visual cue can help you to remain focused on your goal."

"Sure do! I keep hearing how challenging the journey will be, so it'll be important to stay positive."

"Speaking of positivity, have you read the book *The Power of Positive Thinking*, by Norman Vincent Peale?"

"No, why?"

"He's considered to be one of the great authorities on positive thinking. Personally, I really enjoyed the book—he talks about the power of faith and how it can impact success. You might hear some high-performance coaches discredit the theory, arguing that positive thinking without a specific goal or action isn't effective as a success strategy. I suppose that argument is like the limitation we were just discussing of visualization—visualization without action won't move you closer to success either. I'll leave it up to you to decide."

Alex stood up and paced around his living room. "I'm getting the idea that this entrepreneurial journey isn't a science. We've talked about different techniques for staying motivated, like goal setting, visualization, and positive thinking. It feels like a lot of emotional preparation for the journey. Have I got that right?"

Alex could hear the smile in Janine's voice. "Yes, you are the architect of your journey. As an entrepreneur, you are empowered to design the life you want. But if you haven't clearly defined what that vision is, you won't make that happen."

Alex continued to pace. "That's both empowering and frightening at the same time."

"Look, I was in your shoes not long ago. I was excited about starting a business, but I wasn't as clear as I thought about my vision. That's another example of a lesson I needed to learn the hard way."

"How so?"

"I've told you before that one of the reasons why I quit my full-time corporate position was to be able to do more traveling, but because I wasn't very clear about my vision for travel, I was a terrible boss! Remember how I told you before that I didn't give myself a vacation for almost a year?" They both laughed. "Seriously. I never clearly defined what more travel meant—how many trips each year, for how many weeks, and at what times during the year. As a result, I got busy starting the business, and fell into a bad habit of not planning any trips."

Alex shook his head, chuckling. "That's right—you did mention that traveling was your compelling why. Boy— you were an awful boss. Didn't you say you had a picture of Italy on your wall as a reminder?"

Janine shook her head. "Actually, no, I didn't have that picture of Italy posted on my wall at that point. The picture only came AFTER I had the wake-up call that I needed a reminder to always have a vacation planned. Now I'm in a routine of picking my next vacation spot when I return from each trip. That's part of the culture map I created."

Alex stopped pacing. "Culture map? What's that?"

"Sorry Alex, but I've completely lost track of time. I'm late for an appointment."

"Oh—sorry to keep you talking for so long."

"Listen, why don't we pick this topic up again in my office, and I'll show you the culture map. It's better that you see it in person anyway."

Janine and Alex made plans to meet on Friday morning.

Lesson 10 Summary

Key Takeaways:

There are several mistakes that startup owners make with respect to goal setting:

- They make the mistake of not setting a goal, which causes them to drift, get discouraged by the lack of progress, and quit
- They make the mistake of not setting milestones that can be used to assess their progress, which provide valuable feedback to recalibrate their course if needed
- They make the mistake of not celebrating their successes—patting themselves on the back when there is no one else around to do it
- They make the mistake of not aligning their calendar with their ideal schedule—blocking off times, days, and weeks when they are not available
- They make the mistake of not writing down their goal, which can drive accountability
- They make the mistake of not sharing their goal with an accountability partner who will 'nudge' them when they're not following through on their commitment to themselves
- They make the mistake of broadcasting their goal to skeptical family, friends, or strangers on social media who may respond negatively

- They make the mistake of not using the power of visualization, positive thinking, or a trigger such as a picture or sticky notes as a reminder to stay focused on their polar star

Design the life you want, and don't let anyone kill your dream!

Question to Consider:
What is your polar star or goal for your business?

Part D:
Wrapping up

Introducing the 4D Culture Map

"Alex, the copy of my 4D culture map is hanging on the wall in my office. Why don't you go have a look at it, while I grab some coffee for us."

When Janine arrived a few minutes later, Alex was standing in front of the oversized map on the wall. She placed the coffee on a small round table next to the map before sitting down in one of the two chairs.

"I see you found the 4D culture map without any trouble."

Alex stretched out his hands. "How could I miss it—it takes up a third of the wall!"

"Oh, you're exaggerating!"

When Alex turned around, Janine could see that Alex was grinning from ear to ear. "I love it! Thanks for sharing this with me. You've described the culture of your business in one page!"

"That's the purpose of the one-page 4D culture map. You see, my first experience with running a business taught me that I wasn't prepared for the entrepreneurial journey. I learned the importance of being INTENTIONAL about architecting the life that I wanted when starting up a business. The purpose of this culture map template is to provide my clients with a practical guide for designing the right work environment where they will thrive—that includes the workplace, their work habits, and the workforce who will be supporting them, regardless of whether they are internal employees or external contingent workers."

Alex grabbed the notebook and pen from his backpack and sat down on the empty chair. "I've got to make some notes. We've talked about employee engagement but not the notion of entrepreneur engagement."

"Like I said in the coffee shop, most people can articulate what they don't like about their corporate work environment, but they struggle to describe what they DO want. Failure to create a vision for your ideal workplace can result in falling into the trap of 'accidental disengagement,' which is a situation where we're unintentionally creating a disengaging work environment for ourselves. Like the mistake I made when I wasn't giving myself any vacation time for travel."

Alex wrote down the words, *accidental disengagement = unintentional disengaging work environment.* "Sounds like the lesson you learned inspired you to create a useful framework."

"It sure did! And through several conversations with Mark and Lucy, I created the framework that my clients use to populate their 4D culture map."

"I'm not surprised to hear that you collaborated with Mark and Lucy on the framework—I learned so much from them both after only one brief meeting. So, what are the 4 D's?"

The First D is Design

Janine started. "The first D stands for Design. The first step in the framework is to design your own corporate culture, by asking yourself what your ideal work environment looks like. In this section, the three main categories that you're considering are:

1) Where will you work: the physical workplace.

2) How will you work: your work routine.

3) Who will you work with: the people you will be surrounded by, which might include part-time or full-time employees, or any external resources who support you like freelance writers or a technology contractor."

Alex looked over at the 4D culture map and jotted down the three headings that Janine mentioned: Where I Work, How I Work, and Who I Work With.

Janine paused for a moment to let Alex get it all down. "Under each of those headings, I have questions that I use for prompts to help my clients complete each section. For example, under the heading Where I Work, you will ask yourself questions like, 'Where do you do your best work?' 'What is your ideal office setup?' and 'What's in your workspace?'"

Alex was excited. "Those are great questions—let me get those down too."

Janine shook her head. "Don't worry about writing the questions down—I'll send you the framework and the questions afterward. Let's just talk through the rationale for the framework so you understand why each section is important and have some hints about how to complete each one."

"Thanks, that sounds like a good plan! I like the idea of having a structured list of questions as prompts when designing my own corporate culture. In the past, I've done vision boarding exercises where I was told to just write down whatever description comes to mind, with no structure. I don't know how you feel about vision boarding, but I always wonder if there are certain aspects that I overlooked, so I like the categories and specific questions for reflection."

Janine smiled. "Like you, I prefer a structured approach. As you're answering the questions in each of the three sections, you'll want to consider any dissatisfiers or triggers of disengagement for you. I suggest that my clients prepare for the culture mapping by doing a little upfront homework. It's easier to design your ideal work environment when you're looking at a document that summarizes what you DON'T like."

Alex stopped writing and looked up. "When we were in the coffee shop, that's why you suggested that I capture the learnings from my current work experience?"

"You got it! If you completed that task after our meeting, then you've done your homework. At a minimum, I suggest that my clients leverage those learnings to inform the design of their future work environment. That doesn't mean they should be limited by what's on the list—rather, it's a great place to start."

"That's awesome! I'm ready to complete the questions in those three columns. What's the second D?"

The Second D is Detach from Limiting Beliefs and Identity

Janine took a sip of her coffee while deciding how to start this topic. "After you've completed that first D, you'll have a clearer picture of the kind of culture you want to create. But one of the reasons why some startup owners aren't successful is that they have limiting beliefs or an old identity that gets in the way."

"What do you mean?"

"You see, our beliefs affect our expectations, which in turn drives our actions or behavior. So if you have beliefs that are limiting your potential, that's going to affect your results. Let me give you an example. When I was growing up, I recall hearing my parents say things like 'count your pennies,' or 'too much money is a sign of greed.' If your folks had similar expressions, you might still be holding on to those beliefs today, and that's going to affect your expectations of how much money you should earn from the business. When we reach a certain level of success, something will kick in, triggering us to sabotage our success, but not deliberately. Our subconscious kicks in, whether we realize it or not, and it affects our behavior. Does that resonate?"

Alex looked pensive. "I think so. My father had a strong ethic. He would say things like, 'The prize goes to the person who works harder,' or 'The early bird catches the worm.' I suppose you could call those limiting beliefs. Now that I'm thinking about the meaning, it seems to suggest that working a longer day is necessarily the answer, and we know that can lead to burnout or exhaustion."

"Those are great examples of limiting beliefs. The goal of this second D is intended to help you detach yourself from them. We can detach by following these two key steps. Step one is identifying the limiting beliefs; and then step two is creating a new empowering belief to replace it. It should be something that fuels your ambition."

Alex jotted down the two steps. "That seems straightforward. So, whenever I hear my dad's voice telling me to work harder, I should tell myself something like, 'Work smarter, not just harder to avoid burnout.'"

Janine smiled. "Nice work! I love it!"

Alex hesitated. "I'm not sure I can think of something inspiring to replace counting pennies. Any ideas?"

Janine thought for a few seconds. "How about something like, 'Count the ways that the business has given me a deeper connection with my family?' The most powerful beliefs that you could create are ones that foster real emotion."

Alex was writing frantically in his notebook. "That's terrific! I'm going to steal that idea."

Janine chuckled. "Be my guest. You should know that I'm oversimplifying a bit how to detach from limiting beliefs and attach to new empowering beliefs. There's more work to do to shift your mindset and undo years of hardwiring in your brain, but those two steps are the key ones to get you started. Well done with those!"

"That's so true! I'm starting to see how much my father's values have influenced how I think about my career and my business, but I really do find this personal development work fascinating, so I think I'm up for the challenge."

"That makes a big difference when you're genuinely interested in learning and willing to do the work to become a better version of yourself. Shifting your mindset can be challenging and takes time because it can be difficult to recognize our own limiting beliefs. That's why you often see culture depicted as an iceberg; so much of what drives our behavior is 'under the water' or not readily apparent."

Alex chuckled. "I'm drawing the picture of the iceberg for my visual cue and reminder."

Janine laughed. "While you're drawing pictures, you might think of drawing a picture of who you believe you are—your identity."

"What? I'm not sure I follow."

"In this section of your culture map, you'll be identifying both your old beliefs as well as your old identity. Think about how you would describe your identity in your career today, and what you want your identity to be in the future when you start a business."

Alex sat up straight. "Oh! I hadn't thought about it in those terms. How do you describe yourself, Janine?"

"I have a funny story about that. About a year after I started my business, I was at a party and in the situation of having to introduce myself. When the person asked me, 'What do you do?' I said, 'I'm a consultant.' Later that night I thought to myself, 'Why did you say you're a consultant? You're not a consultant anymore.'"

"Interesting! Why do you think you answered that way?"

"At that moment, I realized that I hadn't really shifted my mindset. I hadn't shifted my identity. I suppose it was because one of my businesses involved continuing to do that consulting work for my employer. In my mind, I was still identifying with that role, because it was the role that I've had for over two decades. But in my heart, the role that I'm passionate about is the one that's aligned with my purpose."

Alex leaned forward. "So how did you shift your identity?"

"Well, the first step was to define who I wanted to be. I thought about words like *entrepreneur* and *startup CEO*."

Alex repeated the words, testing them out for himself. "Startup CEO. It has a nice ring to it. It sounds professional, but I'm not sure that I relate to that."

Janine chuckled. "If you conducted a survey of people wanting to start a business to ask them what title they most closely identify with, you would hear a wide range of terms."

"Like what?"

Janine leaned forward. "I mentioned entrepreneur and CEO already. Other terms are sole proprietor, founder, president, managing partner, director, self-employed, contractor, consultant, freelancer and business owner. Off the top of my head, those are the ones I hear most often."

"Wow. I had no idea there could be so many words to mean the same thing. With so many options, which term do you use?"

"Great question. When I'm referring to my clients, I tend to use the term startup owner. The descriptor of startup differentiates the business from established ones, and I find the term owner general enough that no one takes exception to it. I've learned over time that I can easily alienate some startup owners if I call them a CEO or president."

"Ah—makes sense."

"When I'm describing myself, I'm comfortable using the term startup CEO now."

"Did your identity shift as soon as you started calling yourself a startup CEO?"

"No, not exactly. The next step was to ask myself how a startup CEO acts. How should a startup CEO feel? The work was to focus on showing up in a way that I think a startup CEO would show up."

"Is that working?"

Janine smiled. "Yes, on many days. An identity shift doesn't happen overnight, right? But I can honestly say that I'm making progress."

Alex sat back in his chair. "That's amazing. Oh! Let me write that down. That's GOLD!"

The Third D is Document Needs and How to Meet Them

When Janine noticed that Alex had stopped writing, she started again. "Okay, you're ready for the third D, which is to document your needs. You might recall that we touched on this topic."

"Do you mean when we talked about Maslow and his needs framework?"

"That's exactly right. In this section of your 4D culture map, you'll be noting the needs that are most important to you, AND, very importantly, you'll be describing how you plan to meet those with the business."

"Oh! That should be easy. I said that one of my strong desires was to stay connected with Joey until he's off to university. What action should I put next to that? Take Joey to and from school every day, and continue our father/son dialogue?"

"Perfect!"

Alex had a curious look on his face. "But I would do that anyway. Why do I need to write that down?"

Janine shook her head. "You have a great memory—except it's short at times." They both laughed. "It's about being INTENTIONAL. When we're busy running the business, it's easy to fall out of our routine. The next thing you know, you've stopped doing the little things that matter, because it's not always evident that they matter until you stop doing them. Then we feel awful, but we don't even know why we feel that way. Have you ever felt like that before?"

"Okay. That sounded a little complicated but yes, I know exactly what you mean. I used to buy Rachel flowers every other Friday. It would light me up when she came home and saw them on the table at the end of a busy week. I didn't deliberately stop doing that—I just kinda got busy and it slipped my mind."

"Great example! I can see that I don't need to explain how easy it is to fall out of an effective routine. You get it! By writing down the action that you're committed to following through on, you're far less likely to forget, at least until the behavior becomes automatic, like brushing your teeth."

"Hmm. What if Rachel sees that I wrote down the habit of buying her flowers? I can't imagine how she would react."

Janine tried to put herself in Rachel's shoes. "I can't speak for Rachel, but the fact that you wrote down a reminder to yourself to buy flowers doesn't mean that the gesture is any less thoughtful. The fact that you wrote it down means the task is important to you—so much so, that you want to ensure you don't forget."

Alex nodded. "You're absolutely right! I think Rachel would recognize the effort I'm making to remember."

"Good! Then be sure to write that on a sticky note and put it somewhere you look every Friday morning. You're going to need Rachel's support through this journey, so that will be a great habit to resume."

"Did she pay you tell me that?" Alex winked and they both laughed.

The Fourth D is Diarize or Schedule

"All right—you're ready for the last D. The purpose of this fourth D is to increase the likelihood of following through on those actions once you've identified them.

The fourth D is to diarize the actions, or to put them into your schedule or a place where you'll remember to do them. Like the tip I just gave you to write PICK UP FLOWERS on a sticky note where it will be visible on Fridays."

"Okay. That's one example of diarizing. Do you mean I should actually physically write a note in my calendar that says TAKE JOEY TO SCHOOL?"

"Well, has it ever happened that someone has put a meeting in your calendar at eight or eight thirty in the morning, the time when you were planning to take Joey to school?"

"Sure, and when it does, I usually just do the call from the car. Oh! I see where you're going with that. On those occasions when I was on a call, Joey and I didn't have our usual chat."

"Ah! So, if you had blocked off that commuting time in your calendar, how would the situation be different?"

Alex smiled. "You got me! Nine times out of ten, the person would have found a different time in the calendar. It was likely avoidable in most cases."

"Those are the kind of time management tips that Lucy and I discussed when we created the 4D culture map framework. In her research with startup owners, she often discovered that even though the individual said that something was a high priority that month or that week, a review of their calendar often revealed that there was no time blocked off for activities related to that priority."

Alex shook his head. "Really? That surprises me!"

Janine shrugged her shoulders. "We tend to block off time for work priorities, but we tend to be less disciplined blocking off time in the calendar or diary for our personal priorities. And sadly, then we're more likely to lose sight of them. Some people set a reminder on their phone. Figure out what system works for you. The point is that if something is a priority, you'll benefit from scheduling it. Make sense?"

Alex laughed. "Like blocking off times for vacation, perhaps?"

"Smart Aleck...or should I say Smart Alex? Yes. I make a habit NOW of blocking off three weeks in April and three weeks in October—the ideal times of the year to visit Europe. I also block off another two weeks in January, like I mentioned earlier."

"Does that mean you take eight weeks of vacation every year?"

"Well, not exactly. I schedule a three-week block of time knowing that I'll likely take two weeks. I only take five or six weeks, not eight! I guess I still have a little work to do to become a better boss to myself. At least I have self-awareness that I should carve out larger blocks of time in my calendar, knowing that my boss might not approve the whole block."

They laughed.

Alex looked down at his notes and the 4 D's that he had jotted down. *Design the work environment. Detach from limiting beliefs and identify. Document. Diarize.* "Aren't you missing something?"

Janine was puzzled. "What do you mean, Alex?"

"Isn't there a fifth D?" After a few seconds, he added, "Do It."

Janine laughed. "Good point. Just because the activity is in the calendar, that doesn't guarantee it gets done. We need to act."

Alex sat back. "I really like the culture map! This one-pager is a powerful tool for visualizing the kind of business I want to create. Or really, it's the new life I want to architect for myself."

Chapter Summary

Key Takeaways:

The 4D culture map that captures your vision consists of:

- **Design** your ideal work environment—where you will work, how you will work, and who you will work with
- **Detach** from your limiting beliefs and your old identity—replace them with new empowering beliefs and a new identity that is aligned with who you want to become
- **Document** your needs and how the business will enable you to meet them
- **Diarize** your priorities to ensure that your calendar is aligned with your vision for your ideal work environment or culture

Be intentional when designing your ideal life.

Question to Consider:

Are you JUST INTERESTED in starting a business, or are you SERIOUS?

Conclusion

Janine grinned. "I think you're there, Alex. You've learned the secret to fostering an entrepreneurial mindset. Discover your passion. Discover your purpose. Discover your polar star. Then capture that vision in a one-page culture map."

Alex felt the tension release from his shoulders. "I can't thank you enough for sharing the secret to how to get unstuck in my career."

As he left Janine's office, he glanced back at the wall where Janine's 4D culture map was hanging. *I think I'll hang my culture map on the bedroom wall, where I can see it on Monday mornings,* he thought.

Before leaving the parking lot, he pulled the sticky note out of his backpack, pausing for a moment to scan it. *Pick up flowers.* As he placed the note on the dashboard of his car, he felt a surge of excitement and a boost of confidence, knowing he was adopting a new habit on his journey that would shift his mindset forever.

Before backing out of the parking spot, he glanced in his rearview mirror to see if anyone was behind him and caught a glimpse of himself.

He realized that he was grinning from ear to ear—and waited a few seconds to savor the moment.

Summarizing the 10 Lessons and Tips

Lesson 1: **Don't Stay Stuck in a Pity Party of 'What You Want to Move Away From'**

Main Message: The most successful startup owners are resilient. Contrary to what some may believe, most startup owners are not born into the right family, with a silver spoon in their mouths, and they're not the luckiest or the ones who have fewer problems than the rest of us. Quite honestly, they're the ones who have failed most often, because they dare to put themselves out there more than most of us. But when they fail, they first take the learning from the experience, then they move forward by trying again—EVERY time. That's the secret to building resilience.

Advice to Startup Owners: If you're a 'corporate closet dreamer' feeling stuck in your job, leverage the lessons that can be learned from your current work situation—the good, the bad, and the ugly. Do the work to document 'what you want to move away from'—it will serve as a catalyst for shifting your mindset toward the future. When designing the ideal work environment for your startup, you'll have these valuable insights to guide your decisions.

Use the career 'setback' as a 'setup' to find the motivation to start your own business, if that's helpful as a short-term strategy, but don't stay stuck for months, years, or decades in a pity party, a 'victim state,' or focused on revenge.

Lesson 2: Don't Expect to Figure Out Overnight 'What You Want to Move Toward'

Main Message: It's more difficult to figure out what we DO want than to identify what we DON'T want. Successful startup owners are clear about their compelling why—what's motivating them toward business ownership. That clarity helps give them the confidence to take steps toward their entrepreneurial goal. They have the self-awareness to notice if their why is no longer compelling or motivating them. They recognize when they are simply drifting along and they're willing to do the work necessary to discover a new compelling why. Successful startup owners understand that their motivation doesn't always last a lifetime; it often changes as their life circumstances change. That's just part of the learning journey.

Advice to Startup Owners: As a 'corporate closet dreamer,' you know that you're starting to get unstuck in your career when you've stopped focusing on 'what you want to move away from' and start shifting your mindset to 'what you want to move toward.' Recognize that discovering your why is not a science. It's based on FEELINGS, and not FACTS. There isn't ONE right answer, so choose the answer that's right for you TODAY, knowing that it will likely evolve. To discover your why, ask yourself what fuels excitement or passion within you. When that fuel fades, it's time to do the work again to reignite that passion.

Lesson 3: Don't Overlook the Power of 'Wanting to Move Others'

Main Message: It's human nature that we are willing to do more for others than we are willing to do for ourselves. Successful startup owners often talk passionately about wanting to impact others or to leave a legacy behind. According to Maslow, we have a deep need for connection with others—we crave friendship, intimacy, and love. Startup owners who discover a compelling why that taps into this deeply rooted need for connection are more motivated than if they had discovered a why that was focused on their own well-being.

Advice to Startup Owners: If you're struggling to decide between two options for your why, consider choosing the one that involves having a connection with others. You may be motivated to impact your family, friends, co-workers, or a segment of the population who is experiencing something that you have endured. If you're doubting whether your own experience qualifies you to help others who likely resemble an earlier version of yourself, remember that you don't need to be an expert—by sharing your story and lessons learned, you will positively impact another person.

Lesson 4: Don't Confuse Passion and Purpose

Main Message: Although the terms are sometimes used interchangeably, I believe that passion refers to your WHY, whereas purpose refers to your WHAT. The desired outcome as it relates to passion is to achieve motivation—startup owners are driven by their why to establish a business. Conversely, the desired outcome as it relates to purpose is to achieve alignment—startup owners choose an idea for their business that is aligned with their personal purpose. Startup owners who are clear about their passion and their purpose are more successful than those who are not. That's a fact—it's not my opinion.

Advice to Startup Owners: Discover your passion or your why, prior to choosing your what. If you have a compelling reason to start a business, you will have the drive to search for answers on how you will achieve it. When you identify the purpose of your business, choose a business idea that truly excites you to increase the likelihood that the business will be sustainable.

Lesson 5: Don't Stay Stuck in a Misalignment of Your Personal and Business Purpose

Main Message: When successful startup owners define what business they want to be in, they also define what business they DON'T want to be in. By setting up these guideposts, they are more likely to avoid the trap that some startup owners fall into of jumping at the first opportunity that comes along, even though it's not aligned with their purpose. It also helps them to recognize if the work they are doing starts to drift outside of their purpose, which is evidence of misalignment. When the work we're doing is not aligned with our purpose, we tend to quit, as evidenced by the 31% of employees who reportedly left their job due to a lack of meaning.

Advice to Startup Owners: Validate that your business idea is aligned with your purpose before you start. Avoid the temptation to pursue a business idea because you believe it will make you rich or because everyone else on social media seems to be doing it. If you choose a business idea that you are passionate about, and one that allows you to be an authentic and better version of yourself, you have likely discovered your purpose.

Lesson 6: Don't Let Anyone Else Tell You What Your Purpose Should Be

Main Message: Successful startup owners are intentional about the purpose of their business. When choosing a business idea, they don't let others talk them into starting up a business that they're not excited about, even if that other person is well-intentioned. If they realize that they've strayed from their original purpose, they either redirect the business back to its original purpose or may decide to exit that business and start a new one, in order to stay true to their purpose. Successful startup owners evolve their businesses over time deliberately, often with the intention to better serve their clients, rather than in response to peer pressure or 'people pleasing.'

Advice to Startup Owners*:* Before pursuing a business idea that someone else has suggested, validate that you are truly excited about the idea and that it is aligned with your purpose. Don't settle by convincing yourself the idea is 'good enough' or it will be worth doing to make someone else happy if your heart isn't in it. Over time, the business will feel like something that has been done TO DO, not BY YOU. Once you've decided on your business idea, set boundaries around what you're prepared to do and not do.

Lesson 7: Don't Fall into the Trap of Thinking We Have Only One Purpose in Life

Main Message: In today's economy where there are numerous ways to make money, many people are choosing to have a portfolio career, a term that refers to having more than one job or business at a time. Don't believe the bad advice that you need to focus 100% of your time on one business idea. There are countless examples of successful startup owners who have started multiple businesses in their lifetimes—even quite diverse businesses. Chances are there are many topics that you are passionate about, and more than one of them could be a viable business idea.

Advice to Startup Owners: Don't believe the myth that we only have one purpose or calling in life, which can put enormous pressure on you to figure out what your 'one thing' is. If you're not able to start up a business without a source of revenue in the early days, consider a part-time or contract job that will provide a regular paycheck until the business you're starting up begins making money. Starting up more slowly in a part-time capacity or as a 'side hustle' is almost always better than not starting at all.

Lesson 8: Don't Fall into the Common Traps that Contribute to Most Small Business Failures

Main Message: Successful startup owners know that effective business planning is the key to their long-term success—a secret that self-help author Napoleon Hill discovered in his research over 100 years ago. They know that cash flow planning and market research are critical steps of business planning that most people skip, and that these gaps are the top contributors to small business failure. They prepare themselves for entrepreneurship by anticipating the work they'll be doing, how they plan to operate the business, and which skill gaps they need to address to run it effectively, setting them apart from two thirds of all startup owners not willing to do that work.

Advice to Startup Owners: Don't fall into the common trap of thinking that your business planning is complete after developing a marketing plan. Engage in an effective startup business planning process that considers all aspects of the business to give yourself insight into the work that you'll be doing. Assess your ability to do the work effectively—identify areas where you need to build your skills or find talent to fill the gap. Constantly identify mentors who you can learn from. Identify a role model—someone who is running a business that is like the one you want to create and perhaps slightly ahead of you on the journey. Avoid comparing yourself to owners of businesses that are significantly larger to help mitigate imposter syndrome.

Lesson 9: Don't Believe the Fairy Tale About Overnight Success

Main Message: Successful startup owners aren't under any grand illusion that an abundance of wealth can be created overnight. When they hear stories of online influencers who seemingly became famous overnight, they know that the individual did a TON of work behind the scenes—likely for years and maybe even decades, before becoming wealthy. They aren't fooled by pictures of entrepreneurs in their mid-30s standing next to jets, luxury cars, and estates—they know that most billionaires made their money after they turned 50 and most are in their mid-60s. Successful startup owners expect to be agile and willing to evolve their business model, knowing that it may take 10 years or more to figure out the secret formula for financial abundance.

Advice to Startup Owners: Develop a cash flow spreadsheet for your startup business to understand the finances—the money flowing in and out of the business. Document the assumptions upon which the revenue and expense estimates are based. Identify any time periods (months) when you expect to be losing money or incurring a loss, and decide in advance how you will deal with it. Reinvest the profit from the business in the early days, rather than using it to buy that Lamborghini you've always wanted. Set a financial target for your first year to give yourself something to aim at and validate whether your assumptions about the number of units you'll sell and the price you'll charge will enable you to reach your target.

Lesson 10: Don't Be Afraid to Have a Goal or to Define Success

Main Message: Successful startup owners regularly set business goals. They constantly update their goals to ensure that they represent a stretch, which motivates them to reach that next level of performance. Depending on the individual, the nature of the goal may vary widely.

For example, it might be expressed as a financial target, by the desired impact, by the desired size of the business, by how they want clients to perceive them, or by some other measure. Goal-setting decisions are as personal as decisions about passion or purpose.

Advice to Startup Owners: Before starting up a business, set a goal for yourself that stretches and inspires you. Share that goal with an accountability partner if you find it beneficial to have a loved one prompt or nudge you from time to time. Identify a visual cue—perhaps a picture or a written statement—that illustrates that goal to serve as a reminder. As you progress towards that goal, you may find it is no longer a stretch or inspiring—that's your clue that it's time to refresh your goal.

Acknowledgements

I am so grateful to my entire family and the many friends who have supported my entrepreneurial journey. In particular, to my sister—sisters by chance and best friends by choice. As children, Joanne was a royal pain in my butt—a typical older sister. As adults, she is now the kick in my butt that I need from time to time—holding me accountable when she sees me not living up to the promise that I made to myself for this business. To her kids, Nathalie who has contributed her creative talents as a photographer and hairdresser and Justin who has served as my IT department on numerous occasions.

To my brother and his children—Melissa and Nicole, who were my biggest followers (okay admittedly, my only ones) on Instagram in the early days. Without their support, I'm certain I would have abandoned my entrepreneurial journey on one of those lonely days.

A special thank you to my friend Gerry for his constant mentorship over the years, for reviewing multiple versions of this book and tactfully giving me honest feedback, as well as to Judy McBride and Laura

Chavira Razo who both reviewed an early draft and provided invaluable perspectives and feedback. A big thank you to Suzy Vadori, an accomplished author of fantasy books, who provided amazing editorial advice on my first attempt at this book which helped to shape the structure of this book and to Nicole Bross for her strong editorial support. And to my clients—the hundreds of professionals who I've had the privilege to coach. It gives me immense satisfaction to see so many of them still in business over fifteen years later.

About the Author

Janine Lang is a startup coach, writer, online course creator, and the CEO of Agile Business Planning Corp. Janine has been an advisor to corporate executives in the areas of organization design, the talent experience, and corporate culture for over two decades, while working for some of the largest global consulting firms including Accenture, Deloitte, EY, and KPMG. Her client list includes some of the largest companies in Canada and globally, across a wide range of industry sectors.

Her career as an advisor to startup owners began at Hallmark Cards with retailers; in EY's Entrepreneurial Business Centre with technology startups during the dotcom era; in Knightsbridge's entrepreneurship program with downsized professionals wanting to make a career shift to business ownership; in Deloitte's small business practice with CFOs; and in her personal life as a coach to countless entrepreneurial-spirited family and friends. In this last chapter of her career, she is focused on helping the next generation of startup owners to realize their entrepreneurial dreams.

Notes

Introduction

1. "State of the Global Workplace: 2023 Report, The Majority of the World's Employees are Quiet Quitting," Gallup Workplace, Accessed May 25, 2024 at https://www.gallup.com/workplace/349484/state-of-the-global-workplace.aspx.

2. Paolo Confino, "Return to Office Job Satisfaction," Fortune, Accessed May 25, 2024 at https://fortune.com/2024/01/26/return-to-office-job-satisfaction-financial-performance-study/

3. Aaron De Smet et al, "Some Employees are Destroying Value. Others are Building It. Do you Know the Difference?" McKinsey Quarterly, September 11, 2023, https://www.mckinsey.com/capabilities/people-and-organizational-performance/our-insights/some-employees-are-destroying-value-others-are-building-it-do-you-know-the-difference?

4. Raju Narisetti, "What Separates the Best CEOs from the Rest?" McKinsey & Company, December 15, 2021, https://www.mckinsey.com/featured-insights/mckinsey-on-books/author-talks-what-separates-the-best-ceos-from-the-rest.

5. Timothy Carter, "The True Failure Rate of Small Businesses," Entrepreneur Magazine, January 3, 2021, https://www.entrepreneur.com/starting-a-business/the-true-failure-rate-of-small-businesses/361350.

6. Benjamin Hardy, "23 Michael Jordan Quotes That Will Immediately Boost Your Confidence," Inc., Apr. 5, 2016, https://www.inc.com/benjamin-p-hardy/23-michael-jordan-quotes-that-will-immediately-boost-your-confidence.html.

Lesson 1: Don't Stay Stuck in a Pity Party of 'What you Want to Move Away From'

7. Tim Bajarin, "Steve Jobs' Firing From Apple Vs. Sam Altman's Firing From OpenAI," Forbes, Nov. 20, 2023, https://www.forbes.com/sites/timbajarin/2023/11/20/steve-jobs-firing-from-apple-vs-sam-altmans-firing-from-openai/#.
8. Michael Bloomberg, "Corporate firing at the age of 39", Instagram post. May 25, 2024. https://www.instagram.com/mike.bloomberg?igsh=czJzMGJqeXF5bTc0.

Lesson 3: Don't Overlook the Power of 'Wanting to Move Others'

9. Wikipedia, s.v. "Maslow's Hierarchy of Needs," Accessed on April 18, 2024, https://en.wikipedia.org/wiki/Maslow%27s_hierarchy_of_needs.
10. Ibid.
11. Ibid.
12. Ibid.

Lesson 4: Don't Confuse Passion and Purpose

13. Carolyn Dewar et al., "The mindsets and practices of excellent CEOs," McKinsey & Company, Oct. 25, 2019, https://www.mckinsey.com/capabilities/strategy-and-corporate-finance/our-insights/the-mindsets-and-practices-of-excellent-ceos.
14. Rick Warren, "TED Talk: A Life of Purpose & What's in Your Hand," Christian Marriage Spice, Accessed on April 18, 2024, https://www.christianmarriagespce.com/paster-rick-warrens-ted-talk-a-life-of-purpose-whats-in-your-hand/
15. Anthony Trucks' online presentation delivered as part of his Mindset, Resilience & Identity Challenge, accessed on the GrowthDay App, produced by Brendon Burchard.
16. Jim Collins, Good to Great (New York: HarperCollins Publishers, Inc. 2001), Pg. 91.

Lesson 5: Don't Stay Stuck in a Misalignment of Your Personal and Business Purpose

17. Aaron De Smet et al, "The Great Attrition is making hiring harder. Are you searching the right talent pools?" McKinsey Quarterly, July 2022, https://www.mckinsey.com/capabilities/people-and-organizational-performance/our-insights/the-great-attrition-is-making-hiring-harder-are-you-searching-the-right-talent-pools

18. Ibid.

19. Ibid.

20. Ibid.

21. Ibid.

22. Ibid.

Lesson 7: Don't Fall Into the Trap of Thinking We Have Only One Purpose in Life

23. I have chosen a number of well-known entrepreneurs who have multiple businesses. Oprah Winfrey has numerous businesses including TV network, magazine, and radio companies; Elon Musk's businesses include Tesla, SpaceX, and PayPal; Tony Robbins owns over 100 businesses in the personal development, health and wellness, and financial services industries; and Jeff Bezos, who owns Amazon, The Washington Post, and Whole Foods.

24. Charles Handy, The Empty Raincoat: Making Sense of the Future (London: Arrow Books, 1995).

25. "The US Gig Economy," Staffing Industry Analysts, September 23, 2022, https://www2.staffingindustry.com/Research/Research-Reports/Americas/The-US-Gig-Economy-2022-Edition.

26. Sania Khan, "The Contingent Workforce is About to Skyrocket--Here's What You Need to Know," Eightfold AI, February 2, 2023, https://eightfold.ai/blog/the-contingent-workforce-is-about-to-skyrocket-here's-what-you-need-to-know/

27. Ibid.

28. Greg Heywood, "Contingent Workers What are They? What Do You Owe Them?" PeopleTalk, June 6, 2020, https://peopletalkonline.ca/contingent-workers-what-are-they-what-do-you-owe-them/.

29. "Workforce Shaping is HR's Defining Challenge," KPMG International, Pg. 9.

Lesson 8: Don't Believe the Fairy Tale About Overnight Success

30. Dennis Jacobe, "Work is Labor of Love for Small-Business Owners," Gallup News, August 23, 2005, https://news.gallup.com/poll/18088/work-labor-love-small-business-owners.aspx

31. Stephanie, "Building a Business is a 7-10 Year Journey," TalkRoute, Accessed May 25, 2024 at https://talkroute.com/building-business-is-7-10-year-journey/.

32. Nathan Olivarez-Giles, "Tesla Turns First Profit in its 10-Year History," The Verge, May 8, 2013, https://www.theverge.com/2013/5/8/4313442/tesla-turns-first-profit.

33. Madeline Berg, "Billionaires are older than you may think," Business Insider, June 2, 2023, https://www.businessinsider.com/age-billionaire-older-than-you-think-not-young-2023-6?amp

34. Ibid.

35. Susan Guillory, "How to Keep Your Business Partnership From Imploding," Forbes, March 13, 2019, https://www.forbes.com/sites/allbusienss/2019/03/013/keep-business-partnership-from-imploding/?sh=697386717338

36. Ibid.

37. Ibid.

Lesson 9: Don't Fall into the Common Traps that Contribute to Most Small Business Failures

38. Timothy Carter, "The True Failure Rate of Small Businesses," Entrepreneur Magazine, January 3, 2021, https://www.entrepreneur.com/starting-a-business/the-true-failure-rate-of-small-businesses/361350.

39. Carolyn Dewar et al., "The mindsets and practices of excellent CEOs."

40. Lauchlan Mackinnon, "How Many Entrepreneurs Write a Business Plan?" LinkedIn, April 24, 2019, https://www.linkedin.com/pulse/how-many-people-write-business-plan-lauchlan-mackinnon-ph-d-/

41. Carolyn Dewar et al., CEO Excellence: The Six Mindsets that Distinguish the Best Leaders from the Rest (New York: Simon & Schuster, Inc. 2022) Pg. 11

42. Ibid. Pg. 10

43. Ibid. pg. 14

44. Ibid. Pg. 11

45. Ibid. Pg. 11

46. Tony Robbins' virtual Time to Rise Summit event on January 25, 2024.

47. Larry Shaffer, "You really can learn as much from failure as you do success," Fast Company, June 19, 2022, https://www.fastcompany.com/90761446/you-really-can-learn-as-much-from-failure-as-you-do-success.

Lesson 10: Don't Be Afraid to Have a Goal or to Define Success

48. Denzel Washington, "Dreams without goals are just dreams", Instagram Post. May 27, 2024. https://www.instagram.com/reel/C7K537ko4bD/?igsh=Y2gyOWV6dDRsdHgy.

49. Zig Ziglar—Quotes, "If you aim at nothing, you will hit it every time", Accessed April 18, 2024. https://www.instagram.com/thezigziglar?igsh=MXFraWoweG5temEQNQ==.

50. There were no specific references used to develop the description of visualization or its benefits. The author is aware of athletes who have used the techniques effectively.

References

Bajarin, Tim. "Steve Jobs' Firing from Apple Vs. Sam Altman's Firing from OpenAI." Forbes. November 20, 2023, https://www.forbes.com/sites/timbajarin/2023/11/20/steve-jobs-firing-from-apple-vs-sam-altmans-firing-from-openai/#.

Berg, Madeline. "Billionaires are older than you may think." Business Insider. June 2, 2023. https://www.businessinsider.com/age-billionaire-older-than-you-think-not-young-2023-6?amp.

Bloomberg, Michael. "Corporate firing at the age of 39", Instagram post. May 25, 2024. https://www.instagram.com/mike.bloomberg?igsh=czJzMGJqeXF5bTc0.

Carter, Timothy. "The True Failure Rate of Small Businesses." Entrepreneur Magazine. January 3, 2021. https://www.entrepreneur.com/starting-a-business/the-true-failure-rate-of-small-businesses/361350.

Collins, Jim. Good to Great. New York: HarperCollins Publishers, Inc., 2001.

Confino, Paolo. "Return to Office Job Satisfaction." Fortune. January 2024. https://fortune.com/2024/01/26/return-to-office-job-satisfaction-financial-performance-study/.

De Smet, Aaron, et al. "Some Employees are Destroying Value. Others are Building It." McKinsey Quarterly. September 11, 2024. https://www.mckinsey.com/capabilities/people-and-organizational-performance/our-insights/some-employees-are-destroying-value-others-are-building-it-do-you-know-the-difference.

De Smet, Aaron, et al. "The Great Attrition is making hiring harder. Are you searching the right talent pools?" McKinsey Quarterly. July 2022. https://www.mckinsey.com/capabilities/people-and-organizational-performance/our-insights/the-great-attrition-is-making-hiring-harder-are-you-searching-the-right-talent-pools

Dewar, Carolyn, et al. CEO Excellence: The Six Mindsets that Distinguish the Best Leaders from the Rest. New York: Simon & Schuster, Inc., 2022.

Dewar, Carolyn et al. "The mindsets and practices of excellent CEOs." McKinsey & Company. October 25, 2019. https://www.mckinsey.com/capabilities/strategy-and-corporate-finance/our-insights/the-mindsets-and-practices-of-excellent-ceos.

Gallup. "State of the Global Workplace: 2023 Report. The Majority of the World's Employees are Quiet Quitting." Gallup Workplace, 2023. https://www.gallup.com/workplace/349484/state-of-the-global-workplace.aspx.

Guillory, Susan. "How to Keep Your Business Partnership from Imploding." Forbes. March 13, 2019. https://www.forbes.com/sites/allbusienss/2019/03/013/keep-business-partnership-from-imploding/?sh=697386717338.

Hardy, Benjamin. "23 Michael Jordan Quotes That Will Immediately Boost Your Confidence." Inc. April 5, 2016. https://www.inc.com/benjamin-p-hardy/23-michael-jordan-quotes-that-will-immediately-boost-your-confidence.html .

Heywood, Greg. "Contingent Workers What Are They? What Do You Owe Them?" PeopleTalk. June 6, 2020. https://peopletalkonline.ca/contingent-workers-what-are-they-what-do-you-owe-them/.

Jacobe, Dennis. "Work is Labor of Love for Small-Business Owners." Gallup News. August 23, 2005. https://news.gallup.com/poll/18088/work-labor-love-small-business-owners.aspx.

Khan, Sania. "The Contingent Workforce is About to Skyrocket--Here's What You Need to Know." Eightfold AI. February 2, 2023. eightfold.ai/blog/the-contingent-workforce-is-about-to-skyrocket-here's-what-you-need-to-know/

KPMG International. "Workforce Shaping is HR's Defining Challenge" that appeared in the white paper entitled Future of HR 2020: Which Path Are You Taking? 2020.

Mackinnon, Lauchlan. "How Many Entrepreneurs Write a Business Plan?" LinkedIn. April 24, 2019. https://www.linkedin.com/pulse/how-many-people-write-business-plan-lauchlan-mackinnon-ph-d-/

Narisetti, Rajul. "What Separates the Best CEOs from the Rest?" McKinsey & Company: Author Talks series. December 15, 2021. https://www.mckinsey.com/featured-insights/mckinsey-on-books/author-talks-what-separates-the-best-ceos-from-the-rest.

Olivarez-Giles, Nathan. "Tesla Turns First Profit in its 10-Year History." The Verge. May 8, 2013. https://www.theverge.com/2013/5/8/4313442/tesla-turns-first-profit.

Peale, Norman Vincent. The Power of Positive Thinking. New York: Prentice-Hall, Inc., 1952.

Robbins, Tony. Time to Rise Summit Virtual Event, January 25, 2024.

Shaffer, Larry. "You really can learn as much from failure as you do success." Fast Company. June 19, 2022. https://www.fastcompany.com/90761446/you-really-can-learn-as-much-from-failure-as-you-do-success.

Staffing Industry Analysts. "The US Gig Economy." September 2022. https://www2.staffingindustry.com/Research/Research-Reports/Americas/The-US-Gig-Economy-2022-Edition.

Stephanie (no last name given). "Building a Business is a 7-10 Year Journey." TalkRoute. Accessed May 25, 2024 at https://talkroute.com/building-business-is-7-10-year-journey/

Trucks, Anthony. Mindset, Resilience & Identity Challenge presentation, GrowthDay App, April 2024.

Warren, Rick. "TED Talk: A Life of Purpose & What's in Your Hand." Christian Marriage Spice web site, April 18, 2024, https://www.christianmarriagespce.com/paster-rick-warrens-ted-talk-a-life-of-purpose-whats-in-your-hand/.

Washington, Denzel. "Dreams without goals are just dreams", Instagram Post. May 27, 2024. https://www.instagram.com/reel/C7K537ko4bD/?igsh=Y2gyOWV6dDRsdHgy

Wikipedia. Maslow's Hierarchy of Needs, April 18, 2024. https://en.wikipedia.org/wiki/Maslow%27s_hierarchy_of_needs.

Ziglar, Zig—Quotes, "If you aim at nothing, you will hit it every time", Accessed April 18, 2024. https://www.instagram.com/thezigziglar?igsh=MXFraWoweG5temEQNQ==

Printed in the USA
CPSIA information can be obtained
at www.ICGtesting.com
CBHW071526250824
13581CB00027B/272/J